A
FRONT-ROW
GUIDE TO
RUGBY
UNION CLUBS
THE FIRST DIVISION

A
FRONT-ROW
GUIDE TO
RUGBY
UNION CLUBS
THE FIRST DIVISION

WRITTEN AND ILLUSTRATED
BY DICK TYSON

FOREWORD BY GARETH CHILCOTT

STANLEY PAUL
LONDON

IN ASSOCIATION WITH UMBRO INTERNATIONAL

Stanley Paul & Co. Ltd.

An imprint of Random Century UK Limited
20 Vauxhall Bridge Road, London SW1V 2SA

Random House Australia (Pty) Ltd
20 Alfred Street, Milsons Point, Sydney 2061

Random House New Zealand Limited
18 Poland Road, Glenfield, Auckland

Random House South Africa (Pty) Ltd
PO Box 337, Bergvlei 2012, South Africa

First published 1992

Set in Futura

Printed and bound by BPCC Hazells Ltd

A catalogue record for this book
is available from the British Library

ISBN 0 09 177538 8

Dedicated to the Front-Row Union

ACKNOWLEDGEMENTS

Hello there. Do you know what 'Acknowledgements' means?
Well, 'Acknowledgements' is a very long word which is just another
way of saying, 'Thank you for helping me with my book,'
and this is a very long list of all the people who did just that.

John Griffiths

Author of *British Lions, The Book of English International Rugby,
The Phoenix Book of International Rugby Records,*
and statistical editor of *The Rothman's Rugby Yearbook.*

This man knows a thing or two about rugby.

I am very grateful to him, not only for writing the fascinating club
histories and compiling the statistics that follow,
but also for allowing me to blunder about in his home, raid his
archive material, and use most of it in this book.

He is, unfortunately, Welsh.

Mick Cleary

Writer, both for *The Observer* and *Rugby World and Post.*

This is a man who understands rugby players.

I would like to thank him for persuading the forwards to talk to him
about their dark and dangerous jobs. I would also like to thank him
for painstakingly translating the results into comprehensible English.

He is, unfortunately, Irish.

Dave Urwin

Ex-advertising writer, now all-round Apple™ Macintosh™ genius.
This man knows a thing or two about drinking – but somehow,
when we were sober enough, we sat down and cobbled
this whole book together. He is totally responsible for any misteaks.

Nick Chesworth

Fly half – Cambridge University, Bedford, London Scottish,
Rosslyn Park, The Bitter and Twisted Club (see page 27), etc etc.
This man knows a thing or two about looking disgustingly fit and
healthy. By day he is a marketing man, and gave me some
valuable advice at both the beginning and the end of this project.

I hate to think what he gets up to at night.

Her indoors

Advertising Account Manager. Lynne knows a thing or two about
holding down a proper job and supporting me whilst
I muck around writing and drawing silly books. I owe her everything.
(But she still gives me pocket money.)

Roddy Bloomfield and Dominique Shead

Publishers. These people know a thing or two about taking
the bare bones of an idea and hanging some flesh on it.
To say I'm grateful for their help and enthusiasm would be
like saying I'm grateful for their help and enthusiasm. Which I am.

Dennis Keen

Author of *The Rugby Lions.* This man knows a thing or two
about Rugby F.C., and he very kindly
allowed me to use two pictures from his excellent book.

Bill Cotton

Programme Publications. For allowing me to reproduce so many of
their programme covers in the pages that follow.

Umbro International

I'd like to thank them for their generous support.

The Clubs

I would also like to thank all of the officials at the following clubs for
their help: Bath R.F.C., Bristol R.F.C. (especially Mr. Wynne Jones),
Gloucester R.F.C. (especially Mr. A. Wadley), Harlequins F.C.
(especially Mr. Basil Lambert), Leicester F.C., London Irish R.F.C.
(especially Mr. Mike Flatley), London Scottish F.C. (especially
Mr. John Grecian), Northampton F.C. (especially Mr. Brian Barron),
Orrell R.U.F.C. (especially Mr. Fred Holcroft), Rugby F.C. (especially
Mr. Roy Batchelor), Saracens F.C. (especially Mr. Bill Edwards and
the Saracens Press Office), Wasps F.C. and West Hartlepool R.F.C.
(especially Mr. Les Smith).

The pictures

BATH: Team and action: *Colorsport.* BRISTOL: Team: *Bristol R.F.C.,*
Action: *Neil Elston.* GLOUCESTER: Team: *Richard Ellis at Old Town
Studio,* Action: *Colorsport.* HARLEQUINS: Team and action: *Colorsport.*
LEICESTER: Team: *Rory Underwood and Peter Hallas.* Action:
Colorsport. LONDON IRISH: Team: *Colorsport,* Action: *Colorsport
and Russell Cheyne at Allsport.* LONDON SCOTTISH: Team and
action: *London Scottish F.C.* NORTHAMPTON: Team: *Damien
McFadden,* Action: *Mark Thomson.* ORRELL: Team: *Wigan Observer,*
Action: *Colorsport.* RUGBY: Teams: *Rugby Observer & Rugby F.C.*
Action: *Mike Brett.* SARACENS: Team: *John Townsend,* Action: *Dan
Smith (B/W) and Colorsport (Colour).* WASPS: Team: *Wasps F.C.*
Action: *Picturesport Associates Ltd.* WEST HARTLEPOOL: Team: *Picture
Gallery,* Action: *Mike Brett.* ARCHIVE MATERIAL: *John Griffiths.*

Those big men with no ears

Finally, thanks in advance to front-row forwards everywhere
for the good humour and restraint that I hope to God
they will show me after the publication of this book.

ABOUT THE AUTHOR

This is my first book, and drawing it
really made my wrist ache.

CONTENTS

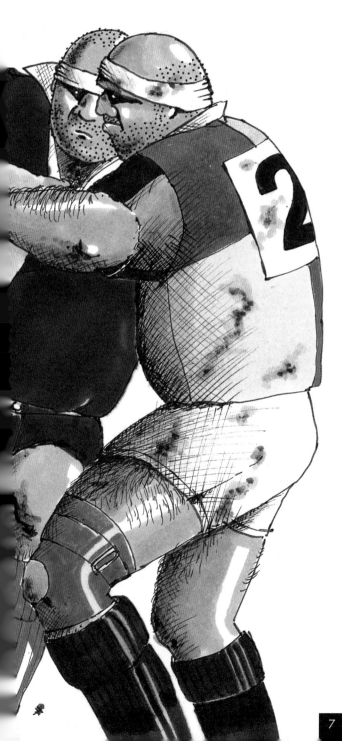

A MAGNIFICENT PAIR OF BRISTOLS, BROUGHT TO YOU COURTESY OF UMBRO INTERNATIONAL

UMBRO INTERNATIONAL LIMITED, P.O. BOX 33, DALLIMORE ROAD, ROUNDTHORN INDUSTRIAL ESTATE, WYTHENSHAWE, MANCHESTER M23 9GJ

AUTHOR'S NOTE

This is a book of two parts. Each club has been allotted four pages – the first of which have been written in an easy-to-understand 'Janet and John' style, ideally suited to the well-known limited literary capabilities of your average front-row forward.

The second two pages on each club are aimed at more literate rugby followers, and I strongly recommend that front-row forwards only tackle these sections in the company of a responsible adult to avoid the frustration (and sometimes the resulting violence) that walks hand in hand with incomprehension.

As is well known, all forwards acquire, sooner or later, the desire to read, and the precise moment when formal instruction in reading should begin rests with the forward himself. Without his interest and co-operation no progress can be made, for the task confronting him is stupendous.

I remember the first time I read the first parts of 'A Front-Row Guide to Rugby Union Clubs' again and again to an enormous tight-head prop forward of my acquaintance.

The pictures illustrated the words perfectly, and were of sufficient appeal to hold his attention every time. In the beginning he asked me to explain certain words, but once their meaning had been assimilated he made them his own.

When the pictures had become entirely familiar to him, he wanted to follow the text, insisting that I should point it out with my finger, word for word. Soon he knew the book so well that he stopped me (usually with a vicious head-high tackle) if I missed or misread any word.

Finally, he would pretend to read the first parts of the book himself. He would say the words out loud, following the text with his enormous finger. He wasn't really reading, but he had learned the *motions* of reading, and no doubt could identify frequently recurring words such as 'try,' 'and,' 'the,' 'pub' etc.

Without giving much consideration to the matter, a warden or psychiatric nurse confronted with this spectacle of a front-row forward *appearing* to read 'A Front-Row Guide to Rugby Union Clubs' might consider it a good book for teaching actual reading skills. Unfortunately, this is far from being the case.

Certain facts, however, will 'stick.' He will learn, for instance, that 'Saracen' is the name of a tank, and that a 'Harlequin' is, in reality, a mute pantomime clown.

But most importantly of all, perhaps, he will learn (just by studying the pictures and maps) such vitally important information as:

* Where to find the opposition's club.
* Where the club bar is.
* How to recognise their players (and indeed, in some pathetically sad cases, his own)
* Where the closest pubs are.

So forget reading skills and let him concentrate on the four points above. After all – when all's said and done, they're all that any forward needs to know.

As for the rest of you, here's your chance to learn a little bit more about English first division rugby union clubs. (Not to mention English first division rugby pubs!)

Dick Tyson

FOR~~E~~W~~O~~RD

BY MR. G.J. CHILCOTT

Forwards these days pride themselves on being able to pass, run, tackle and sidestep. Now you know why I'm thinking of retiring. As for the notion that all forwards are broken-nosed, cauliflower-eared dimwits, I have to say that in my case it's not far off the mark. As for my colleagues, they're all far too intelligent for their own good. When I first began playing, there were only three calls in the book – 'Shove,' 'Hit him' and 'Duck.' Nowadays these boys carry a computer round in their shorts stacked with all the forward variations. So let it be said loud and clear –

FORWARDS ARE NO LONGER THICK.

Again, now you know why I'm thinking of retiring.

I've also heard it said that we're all vicious so and sos in the front-row. Now, I know that I've been sent off five times and that my defence of mistaken identity was wearing a bit thin by the fifth time but, in the main, we are gentle, fun-loving souls. Forwards are without doubt the life and soul of the team. On tours, it's always the donkeys who get out there and do something. Yes, all right it does sometimes go wrong, as happened when the Bath front-row (also known as Beach Whales RFC) went scuba-diving on their Australian tour. Just because Richard Lee went under with his wallet still in his shorts and Graham Dawe tried to get out with his weight belt still around his waist, I just won't have it said that we forwards are a bit short of grey matter. Above all else, we are athletes: 17 stone athletes in my case, but athletes nonetheless. Well, almost.

Gareth Chilcott

Bath time... every front-row forward hates it. Forget about rubber ducks, soap on a rope and a nicely steamed-up pint of beer. All you'll soak up at the Recreation Ground the next time you go is pain. But a trip to Bath does have one thing in common with lying in one. However well you play you'll still be taken to the cleaners.

BATH

So where the hell are they, then?

Get all washed up and cleaned out at the Recreation Ground, Bath, Avon. Tel: 0225 425192.

1. Royal York Tavern
2. Saracen's Head
3. The Oliver
4. The Boater
5. The Rummer
6. The Huntsman Inn
7. The Ale House

Who scores all the points?
(Pull the plug on this lot)

Leading scorers in the League 1991/92
S. Barnes (3 tries, 10 cons, 20 pens, 2dg) 98
J. Webb (8 cons, 12 pens) 52
T. Swift (8 tries) 32, J. Fallon* (7 tries) 28
P. de Glanville (3 tries) 12
Bath's 277 League points included 34 tries.
*Gone North.

How did they do last year?

PLAYED 12 • WON 10 • DRAWN 1 • LOST 1
Points for: 277 • Points against: 126
CHAMPIONS – COURAGE DIVISION ONE
WINNERS – PILKINGTON CUP

Where are the nearest pubs?
See the map.

Where's the bar?

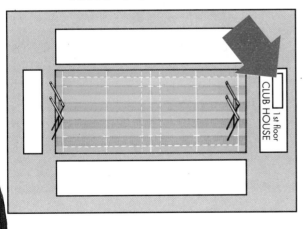

What else?

Founded 1865.
Second XV:
Bath United.

I'VE GOT THOSE WASHDAY BLACK AND BLUES

CHANGE STRIPS

League History: First Division since 1987.
League Honours: First Division Champions 1989, 1991, 1992.
Cup Honours: *Winners* 1984, 1985, 1986, 1987, 1989, 1990, 1992.

Bath were formed in 1865 but did not settle at the Recreation Ground until 1894 when Frank 'Buster' Soane was the outstanding personality at the club. The first international capped for England from Bath, Soane was a skilful forward who skippered his club and county (Somerset) for many years.

Vincent Coates, Ulick Considine and R.A. 'Gerry' Gerrard were Bath players who followed Soane into the England XV. Gerrard was the club's most-capped player until recently and appeared in the centre when England scored their famous victory over New Zealand in 1936. Gerrard, who captained Bath, fell in action in Libya during World War Two, but his wife Molly maintained family ties with the club after the war, serving for many years on Bath's management committee.

In 1950, when Bath-born Arnold Ridley, the author, playwright and actor who portrayed Private Godfrey in *Dad's Army* became club president, Alec Lewis led Bath to a then record season. The club were unbeaten in London, won 13 away matches and 27 altogether. Lewis, whose rugby career had been interrupted by a serious war injury, went on to play for England. Ridley was elected a Bath life member in 1963 in recognition of his services to the club.

England international John Kendall-Carpenter was capped from Bath and inspired the pack in the mid-'50s when John Roberts, who served as player and administrator, was captain. Among the numerous developments off the field during this period leading up to the centenary season were the building of a new stand, the erection of a splendid club house and improvements to players' facilities.

The recent history is of unparalleled success. Always renowned for enterprising back play, the seeds of Bath's triumphs were sown ten years ago. After disappointing

Bath 1991–92: Back row, players only: J. Fallon, S. Ojomoh, M. Haag, N. Redman, B. Clarke, V. Ubogo, J. Mallett, J. Rowell, D. Egerton
Front row: C. Atkins, J. Bamsey, G. Chilcott, R. Hill, J. Webb, J. Guscott, A. Robinson, S. Barnes, P. de Glanville, G. Dawe, T. Swift, S. Knight, I. Lewis.

displays in the old South West Merit Table, they failed to qualify for the RFU cup competition in 1982–83. Then, after an unflattering start to the 1982 season, the imaginative coaching of Jack Rowell began to pay dividends. Rowell encouraged players to enjoy their rugby, even if it meant taking risks. With backs and forwards well versed in the basic skills of the game, the club put together an impressive undefeated run of 26 matches and topped a thousand points in a season for the first time.

A succession of talented outside halves – John Horton, John Palmer and Stuart Barnes – have ignited the team over the past decade. Bath have won the RFU cup seven times and the new Courage League three times, achieving the double twice. In the same period twenty international players wore the club's colours, and there were 15 past, present or future caps in the squad who beat Wasps in the 1987 Cup final.

Bath's phenomenal success has been underwritten by sensible administrators loyal to the club. Jack Simpkins, whose family have been involved with Bath Football Club since the turn of the century, Clive Howard and Tom Hudson all made important contributions. So too have those running the Colts and mini-rugby sections, and it gives the club particular pleasure to point to Jeremy Guscott and say that he began his career with Bath as a seven-year-old.

Above: London Irish 21, Bath 26; 16 November 1991. Gareth Chilcott adding a London Irish jersey to his extensive collection, while Nigel Redman and Richard Hill get on with winning the game.
Above left: Bath 32, Saracens 12; 25 April 1992. We are the champions!
Left: Bath 15, Harlequins 12; Pilkington Cup final, 1992. We are the (yawn) champions… again…
Opposite page: God. And lo, he did mightily smite them and trample them into the very dust from whence they came. Bath 29, Gloucester 9, 29 February 1992.

FACING FORWARDS

No 1: Dave Egerton

Position: N°8 **Age:** 30 **Ht:** 6'5½" **Wt:** 17st

You won't recognise this man when he steps out to play this season. Bath's answer to the Egyptian mummies, Dave Egerton, swathed in bandages from top to toe, is taking no chances this year. Because of injury, he's played barely 25 games in the last two seasons so when the RFU ruled out his plan to play in plaster of Paris, he simply took to the crepe and elastoplast. Watch this man carefully when he's out on the field just in case you catch a glimpse of his famed Gary Glitter impression which wowed the crowds in Lisbon two years ago. He tells jokes – which go down brilliantly in Gloucester – such as: 'What was Terry Waite's first question on release?': 'Are Bath still the best team in the land?' Don't worry either if you forget his name for, being a great fan of Johnny Cash, he'll also answer to the name of Sue. A fun man and a fine player.

Previous clubs
Salisbury, Wasps 3rds (3 games; downhill ever since)
Hobbies
Johnny Cash
Heroes
Roy of the Rovers, Steve Heighway (why is John Barnes called Tarmac? – because he's the black Heighway), Andy Ripley – if I had his body and athleticism I'd be a world beater
Best game
England v Australia '88 (w. 28–19). Billy Beaumont's commentary went: 'great handling movement from the English forwards – Richards, Robinson, Richards to Underwood to score.' He missed me out completely. He obviously didn't know me. Nothing much has changed since
Most enjoyable aspect forward play
Falling over and having a rest
Least enjoyable aspect
So long since played can't remember
Relationship with referees
Platonic
Best tour
England to Australia '88

Best tour story
Argentina 1990.
I was offered a modelling contract of $30,000. It was for a porn mag. A guy approached me after one game and made a broad proposal. I went to meeting in hotel with Mickey Skinner as bodyguard. I passed the audition but Brian Moore later advised me to get a contract. They did a runner. Of course what I was really concerned about was whether the deal contravened the amateurism laws
Favourite drink
A Long Island Iced Tea or a pint of Beamish
Favourite food
Seafood – Blue Whale sandwich in particular
Drinking capacity
Approximately 10 pints, all down in one, a yard of ale and 5 bottles of red wine
Champion drinker
Barnsie
Biggest compliment ever paid
Being overlooked by John Reason
Who I would most liked to have been
One of the Queen's corgis

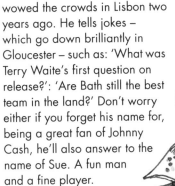

VIRTUTE ET INDUSTRIA

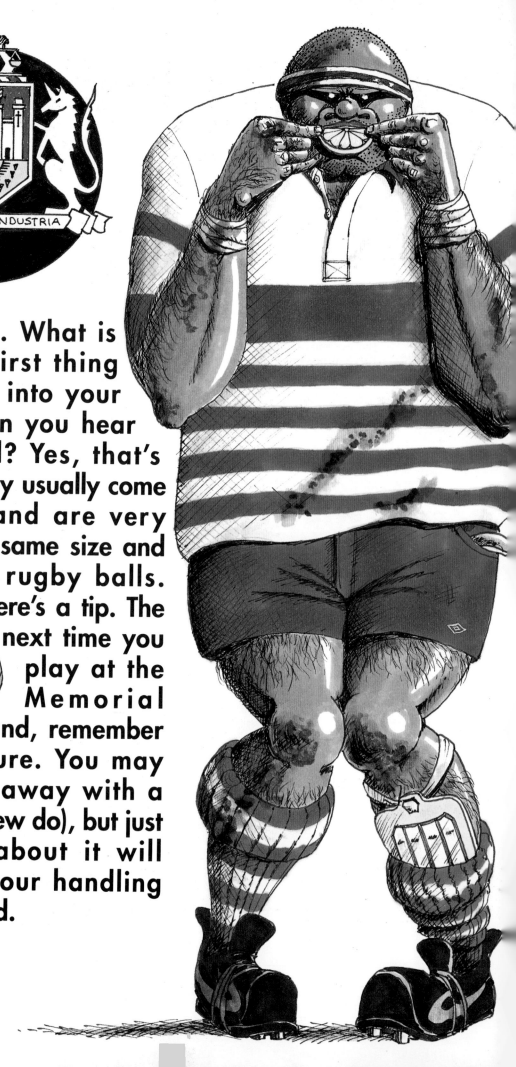

Bristol. What is the first thing that pops into your head when you hear that word? Yes, that's right!!! They usually come in pairs and are very nearly the same size and shape as rugby balls. Here's a tip. The next time you play at the Memorial Ground, remember this picture. You may not come away with a win (very few do), but just thinking about it will improve your handling skills no end.

BRISTOL

Where the hell are they?

Swing low at the Memorial Ground,
Filton Avenue, Horfield, Bristol BS7 0AQ.
Telephone: 0272 514448.

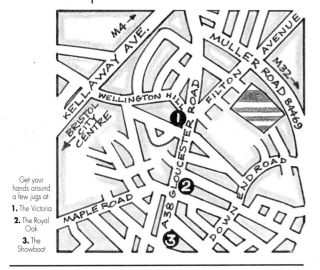

Get your
hands around
a few jugs at:
1. The Victoria
2. The Royal
Oak
3. The
Showboat

Where's the bar?

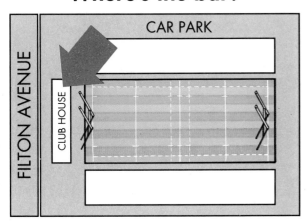

Who scores all the points?

(Keep abreast of this lot)

Leading scorers in the League 1991/92
M Tainton (7 cons, 4 pens, 1dg) 29
P. Hull (2 tries, 2 cons, 5 pens) 27
P. Stiff (5 tries) 20, S. Painter (4 cons, 2
pens, 1dg) 17, J. Davis (4 tries) 16
Bristol's 192 League points
included 29 tries.

How did they do last year?

PLAYED 12 • WON 4 • DRAWN 0 • LOST 8
Points for: 192 • Points against: 174
10TH IN COURAGE LEAGUE ONE

Where are the nearest pubs?

See the map.

What else?

Founded 1888.
Second XV:
Bristol United.

CHANGE STRIP

VIRTUTE ET INDUSTRIA

League History: First Division since 1987.

Cup Honours: *Winners* 1983. *Finalists* 1973, 1984, 1988.

The amalgamation of the Carlton and Redland Park clubs in 1888 represented the foundation of the Bristol Football Club. Despite undertaking an ambitious itinerary in their inaugural season (when there was a defeat by 14 tries to nil at Cardiff in their first game), Bristol's playing strength developed rapidly and in 1891–92 twenty of their twenty-four matches were won.

T.O. Davies and W.T. Pearce, who was also the club's chief administrator, were prominent players of this time, and in 1900 Wallace Jarman became the first Bristolian to be capped by England when he played against Wales.

Up to the Great War, Bristol paid an annual subscription to Gloucestershire County Cricket Club for use of the county ground. During this period more than half a dozen players followed Jarman into the England XV and the RFU, recognising the popularity of the game in the West Country, staged the England–Wales international of 1908 at Ashton Gate, home of Bristol City AFC, though as a spectacle the game was wrecked by thick fog. Undoubtedly the most famous player before World War One was W.R. Johnston, a reliable full-back whose superb defence and flighted kicks served England well in 16 internationals, including two Grand Slams.

Losses suffered during the Great War decimated the playing membership, but in September 1921, thanks partly to generous public subscription, the Memorial Ground was opened at a cost

Bristol 1991–92: Back row: D. Wring, D. John, R. Kitchen, M. Lloyd, H. Duggan, C. Barrow, A. Blackmore, P. Stiff, D. Hinkins, J. Pearson, M. Regan.
Front row: D. Hitton, R. Mibbs, M. Tainton, J. Redcup, P. Hull, D. Eves (Captain), P. Cullings, J. Davies, D. Hickey, A. Lathrope, D. Palmer.

of £26,000. Dedicated to local players who had died in action, the ground vied with Leicester's Welford Road as the best pitch outside London.

In the '20s and '30s brilliant play on the field matched the splendid accommodation off it. Len Corbett, a centre, and Sam Tucker, the first of a line of skilful Bristol hookers to practise their art for England, were loyal clubmen who captained their country. Bristol also acquired a reputation as a trusted nursery for full-backs, three players following Johnston's example acting as the last line of defence for England.

Bristol regrouped quickly after the last war and passed through a Golden Era between 1955 and 1961. John Blake as captain brought a bright approach to the team's play, encouraging backs and forwards to embrace the maxim that attack is the best form of defence. New records for points totals and try scoring were set while crowds flocked in their thousands to the Memorial Ground to watch the club play delightful rugby. There is no better testimony to Bristol's achievements in the period than to quote the playing record:

P 264 W 197 D 12 L 56 For 4066 Against 1882.

Richard Sharp and John Pullin, the club's most-capped player, led England in the '60s and '70s respectively; while the highlight of the past decade was Bristol's Cup final win against Leicester in 1983. With both sides wearing lettered jerseys, Twickenham resembled a life-sized game of Scrabble. Two of Bristol's winning team, Alan Morley and Austin Sheppard, learned the game at Colston's School under the watchful

eye of David Rollitt, another Bristol international. Morley set appearance and try-scoring records for the club.

Despite recent crises of confidence at the Memorial Ground, the successes of West Country rivals can be guaranteed to stimulate a reaction. Nothing unites Bristolians more than the opportunity of toppling Bath!

Above: Bristol 6, Bath 15; Pilkington Cup tie 22 February 1992. Look, mum, no hands – Darryl Hickey practices his levitation skills.
Above left: Bristol cigarette card from the days of hacking (coughs, that is).
Opposite page: T.O. Davies in his natty knitted jersey, circa 1894.

FACING FORWARDS

No 2: Derek Eves

Position: Flanker **Age:** 26 **Ht:** 5' 10" **Wt:** 14st 9lbs

Times have been rather hard down Bristol way these last few seasons. But something is beginning to stir at long last around the Memorial Ground. And nothing stirs quite as dramatically as the squat, dynamic figure of Derek Eves. He talks with that sharp, distinctive Bristol accent; and he tackles with that sharp, distinctive Bristol accent. If they ever get up again, it's considered a failure. Derek Eves is captain of the club. Don't be taken in by his broad smile as he tosses the coin: it's not a sign of welcome. It's the thought of those bruises he's going to inflict over the next 80 minutes.

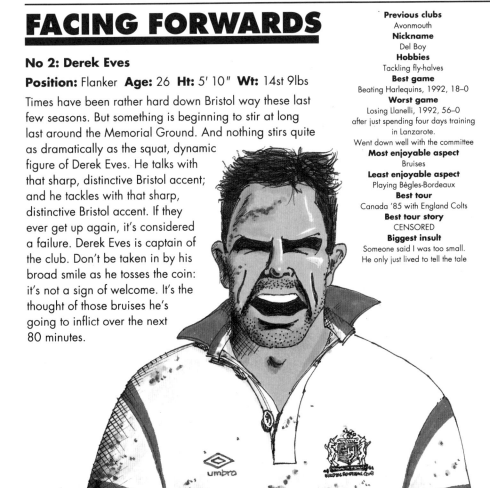

Previous clubs
Avonmouth
Nickname
Del Boy
Hobbies
Tackling fly-halves
Best game
Beating Harlequins, 1992, 18–0
Worst game
Losing Llanelli, 1992, 56–0
after just spending four days training in Lanzarote.
Went down well with the committee
Most enjoyable aspect
Bruises
Least enjoyable aspect
Playing Bègles-Bordeaux
Best tour
Canada '85 with England Colts
Best tour story
CENSORED
Biggest insult
Someone said I was too small.
He only just lived to tell the tale

Least favourite roommate
Peter Stiff,
after several pints of anaesthetic he snores like a pig in a rage
Motto
Go out and enjoy it
Favourite drink
Gin and bitter lemon
Favourite food
Spaghetti bolognaise
Favourite paper
The Sun
Drinking capacity
Up to the horizontal phase
Champion drinker in side
Phil Adams
Most interesting thing about myself
'My body with no clothes on'
– Mrs. Eves
Who I would most liked to have been
Tony O'Reilly – lots of money and lots of rugby

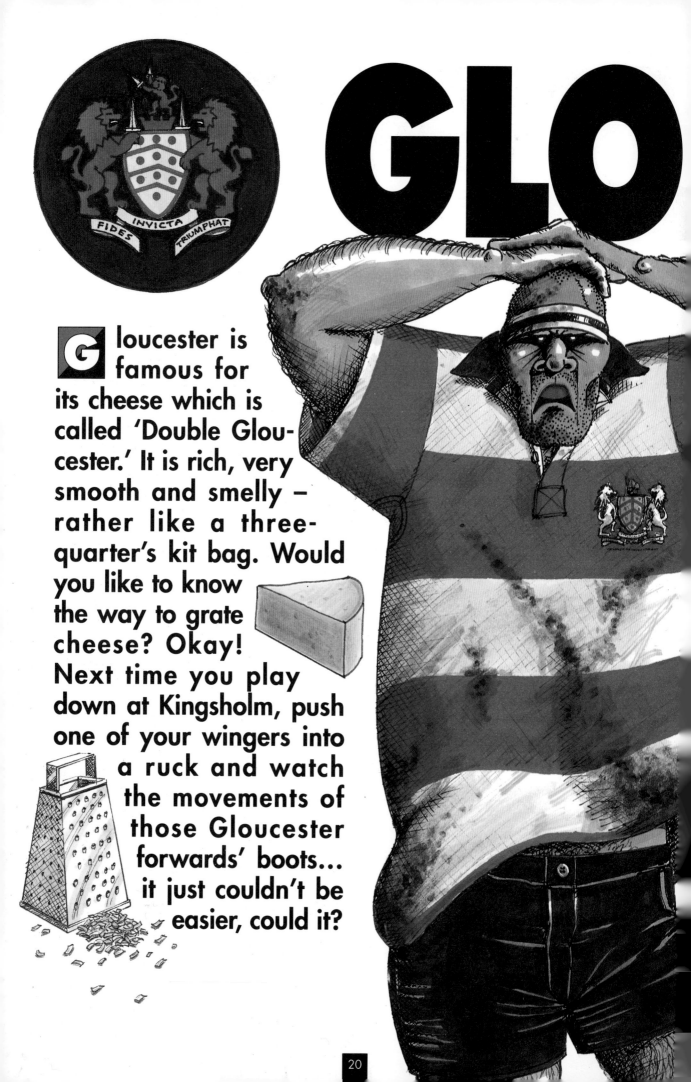

GLO

Gloucester is famous for its cheese which is called 'Double Gloucester.' It is rich, very smooth and smelly – rather like a three-quarter's kit bag. Would you like to know the way to grate cheese? Okay! Next time you play down at Kingsholm, push one of your wingers into a ruck and watch the movements of those Gloucester forwards' boots... it just couldn't be easier, could it?

JCESTER

Where are they?

Kingsholm, Worcester Street, Gloucester. Tel: 0452 520901 or alternatively 0452 528385.

1. Kingsholm Inn
2. The White Hart
3. Queen's Head
4. The Wellington
5. The Welsh Harp
6. England's Glory
7. York House

Where's the bar?

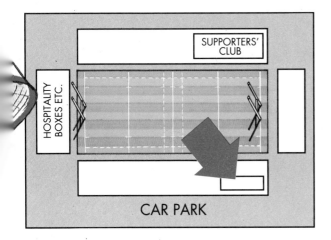

Who scores all the points?
(The Cherry & White blight)

Leading scorers in the League 1991/92
T. Smith (1 try, 10 cons, 19 pens) 81
S. Morris (5 tries) 20, M. Hamlin (4 pens, 1dg) 15, S. Masters (3 tries) 12
M. Roberts (1 con, 3 pens) 11
Gloucester's 193 League points included 20 tries.

How did they do last year?
PLAYED 12 • WON 7 • DRAWN 1 • LOST 4
Points for: 193 • Points against: 168
4TH IN COURAGE LEAGUE ONE

Where are the nearest pubs?
See the map.

What else?
Founded 1865.
Nickname: 'Cherry & Whites'
Second XV: Gloucester Utd.

CHANGE STRIP

League History: First Division since 1987.
Cup Honours: *Winners* 1972, 1978, 1982 (shared).
Finalists 1990.

Tucked away in the *Gloucester Journal* of 15 September 1873 was a brief paragraph heralding the foundation of Gloucester RFC. Forty-five enthusiastic locals met at the Spread Eagle Hotel and for 120 years since, home-grown products have fashioned Gloucester into one of the world's leading rugby clubs. The city has a thriving rugby network comprising 19 junior clubs who jostle to send their finest graduates up to the Gloucester Rugby Football Club.

Innovation was associated with the club in its early years. At a time when rugby matches were a series of protracted forward mauls, Gloucester were pioneers of an open game in which backs and forwards were encouraged to run and pass. The first peak in the club's history was an invincible season in 1882–83 when a strong London combination was beaten by a single try scored by Tommy Bagwell who was promptly deified by rejoicing fans. When the club moved to a new home at

Kingsholm 1891, Bagwell led Gloucester through another successful season.

Bagwell served the club for years after his playing days, acting as coach and general factotum, setting a trend for players turned administrators. Since the First World War, Gloucester RFC have prospered under strong management, and the administrative commitments of three long-serving former players who were internationals – Arthur Hudson, Tom Voyce and Peter Ford – have been invaluable.

There has been a steady procession of Kingsholm men into the England team since the turn of the century. England won the International Championship in 1910 – their first success for 18 years – with four Gloucester men in the side. But the most distinguished player produced by the club was Tom Voyce, an all-action flanker who

> RUGBY FOOTBALL
> UNION
>
> **GLOUCESTER**
>
> v
>
> **MOSELEY**
>
> CLUB KNOCK-OUT COMPETITION
> FINAL
>
> Twickenham   Official Programme
> Saturday   Price 10p
> 29th April 1972

Gloucester 1991–92: Middle row, players only: B. Phillips, P. Jones, M. Hannaford, A. Stanley, S. Masters, N. Scrivens, P. Miles, D. Simms, A. Deacon, B. Fowke, T. Windo, M. Hamlin, N. Marment, D. Cummins, J. Hawker
Front row: N. Matthews, K. Dunn, L. Gardiner, T. Smith, P.J. Ford (Chairman), I. Smith (Captain), Canon H.M. Hughes (President), S. Morris, D. Caskie, I. Morgan, J. Perrins.

Gloucester won the inaugural competition and in the following ten seasons emerged victorious from nearly 75% of their 550 matches, producing numerous internationals and returning to Twickenham for the 1978 and 1982 Cup finals.

Recently, the policy of developing the Colts section has paid handsome dividends. Mike Teague, built like the brick outhouses he constructs as part of his living, has been the outstanding Colt discovery. His storming play for Lions and England has brought much pleasure to Gloucester's loyal supporters.

featured in three England Grand Slam-winning teams during the early 1920s.

Voyce was of such striking appearance, and was such a dynamic forward that is was impossible to mistake him on the field. Once, at the behest of England's selectors, he was told to withdraw from a club match prior to an international. Not wishing to be disloyal to the 'Cherry and Whites' – a nickname derived from the team colours – he decided to play for the club, adopting a pseudonym and disguising himself with a scrum cap. Alas, his subterfuge was rumbled by a local pressman, who began a report of the match with 'Tom Voyce was off-side twice in the first five minutes...'! Voyce won 27 England caps, a club record.

In the '50s and early '60s, Gloucester had to play second fiddle in West country rugby to Bristol. However, the launch of the RFU Cup in 1971–72 coincided with a new dawn in the 'Cherry and Whites' fortunes.

Above: *Gloucester 18, Bath 27. Pilkington Cup tie, 4 April 1992. Kings of Kingsholm, the Gloucester front-row.*
Above left: *In the same game, Dave Simms makes a break, when suddenly: 'Oh, no, it's Ojomo!'*
Opposite page, centre: *How could you disguise a man like this with a mere scrum cap? Tom Voyce, circa 1930.*
Opposite page, top right: *Off to a good start: Gloucester 17, Moseley 6 in the first ever RFU club knockout final, 29 April 1972.*

FACING FORWARDS

No 3: Ian Smith

Position: Open-side flanker **Age:** 29 **Ht:** 6' **Wt:** 14st

Smith and Jones – Tartan names if ever there were two! But it was to Kingsholm that the Scottish selectors trekked last season to fill the gaps in the side. Prop Peter Jones and flanker Ian Smith were just two who discovered a far-flung Scottish granny. Gloucester coach Keith Richardson became known as the coach of the Scottish Development Squad. Smith, though, is a Gloucester man to the bottom of his boots. Gloucester boots have been known to do some walking in their time, usually over opposition forwards who foolishly lie on the ball. Ian Smith, whose father played in a dozen Final English trials, plays his rugby hard but fair.

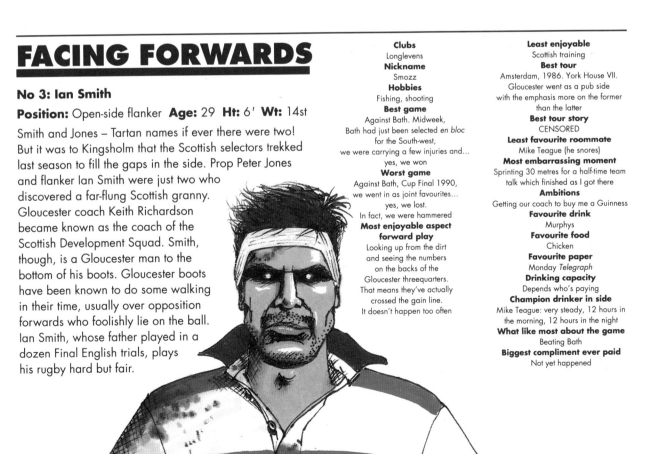

Clubs
Longlevens
Nickname
Smozz
Hobbies
Fishing, shooting
Best game
Against Bath. Midweek, Bath had just been selected *en bloc* for the South-west, we were carrying a few injuries and... yes, we won
Worst game
Against Bath, Cup Final 1990, we went in as joint favourites... yes, we lost.
In fact, we were hammered
Most enjoyable aspect forward play
Looking up from the dirt and seeing the numbers on the backs of the Gloucester threequarters. That means they've actually crossed the gain line. It doesn't happen too often

Least enjoyable
Scottish training
Best tour
Amsterdam, 1986. York House VII. Gloucester went as a pub side with the emphasis more on the former than the latter
Best tour story
CENSORED
Least favourite roommate
Mike Teague (he snores)
Most embarrassing moment
Sprinting 30 metres for a half-time team talk which finished as I got there
Ambitions
Getting our coach to buy me a Guinness
Favourite drink
Murphys
Favourite food
Chicken
Favourite paper
Monday *Telegraph*
Drinking capacity
Depends who's paying
Champion drinker in side
Mike Teague: very steady, 12 hours in the morning, 12 hours in the night
What like most about the game
Beating Bath
Biggest compliment ever paid
Not yet happened

HARL

Harlequins are real pantomime clowns. Did your mum take you to the pantomime this year? If she did you will know that they don't talk, never sleep and are always completely invisible. Unlike the players at the Stoop, who never stop talking, occasionally doze off in the second half and are all highly visible. Especially that bloke William Carling.

Where the hell are they?

The Harlequins play the fools at The Stoop Memorial Ground, Craneford Way, Twickenham, Middlesex. Tel: 081 892 0822.

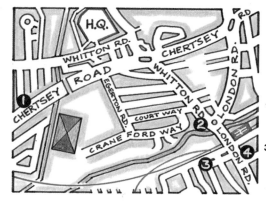

1. The Winning Post
2. The Cabbage Patch
3. The Albany
4. Rugby Tavern

Station: Twickenham

Where's the bar?

EQUINS

Who scores all the points?

D. Pears (4 tries, 15 cons, 21 pens) 109, W. Carling (3 tries) 12, G. Thompson (3 tries) 12, M. Wedderburn (3 tries) 12, Harlequin's 213 League points included 27 tries.

How did they do last year?

PLAYED 12 • WON 5 • DRAWN 1 • LOST 6
Points for: 213 • Points against: 207
8TH IN COURAGE LEAGUE ONE

Where are the nearest pubs?

See the map.

What else?

Founded 1866.
Nickname: 'Quins.'
Second XV: Wanderers

CHANGE STRIP

League History: First Division since 1987.
Cup Honours: Winners 1988, 1991. Finalists 1992.

Since their foundation in 1867, Harlequins have been regarded as the quintessential English rugby club. Matches were originally played on Hampstead Heath and the team wore plain jerseys bearing the monogram HFC – Hampstead Football Club.

In 1869–70, they vacated their field on the Heath, beginning a nomadic existence which lasted some forty years and during which premises were variously occupied at Highbury, Putney, Kensal Green and several west London sites. Then, when the new RFU headquarters were completed in 1909, the club eventually settled at Twickenham, where they have remained ever since.

When the move from Hampstead was made, it was decided to keep the original HFC jerseys to minimise costs. Officials apparently searched the H entries in a dictionary for a suitable substitute name. Harlequin was the word that took everyone's fancy and those wonderful quartered club colours, now recognised throughout the rugby world, were introduced soon after.

By January 1871, the Harlequins had become sufficiently established to be invited to the historic formation of the Rugby Football Union – the only current first division side represented at the foundation meeting.

A.E. Stoddart (who captained England at rugby and cricket) and G.L. Jeffery were among the earliest international players who developed their skills with the 'Quins, and the first Harlequin capped direct from the club was W.R.M. Leake in 1891.

Three distinguished periods of the club's history have coincided with success for the national side. Adrian Stoop, in whose memory the club's current headquarters at Craneford Way is named, was a big influence on Harlequins rugby before the Great War. He was a thoughtful player who believed that accurate passing and imaginative running were key features of effective back play. Around him he gathered skillful

Harlequins 1991–92: **Back row:** *F. Howard (Ref.), A. Harriman, P. Challinor, that bloke William Carling, N. Edwards, P. Ackford, M. Russell, C. Sheasby, M. Hobley, S. Halliday, C. Luxton, P. Thresher.* **Front Row:** *N. Killick, G. Thompson, D. Pears, M. Wedderburn, E. Davis, P. Winterbottom, B. Moore, A. Mullins, R. Glenister, M. Pratley.*

backs – John Birkett, Ronnie Poulton, Douglas Lambert – who practised Stoop's tactics, transforming Harlequins into the most successful club side in England.

In 1910 the English selectors turned to the club for support in the search for long-awaited national success. With Stoop as captain, England beat Wales for the first time in twelve years and the side achieved its first Championship title since 1892. Harlequins appeared in every England team between 1910 and 1913, when the Grand Slam was won, and in 1911 the club's entire threequarter line was selected for the international against

Wales, although two of the players withdrew through injury.

If Stoop was regarded as the father of modern English back play, then Wavell Wakefield, another Harlequin, was the father of modern forward play. He was the first Englishman to insist on specialist scrum positions for forwards and his ideas were incorporated by the England and Harlequins teams of the 1920s. His career as an international included three Grand Slams and he later led Harlequins to wins in the first four finals of the Middlesex Sevens.

Oxbridge Blues and several overseas internationals sustained the club after the last war, but recent successes derived from John Currie's inspired chairmanship of Harlequins in the 1980s. His management and recruitment policies improved standards throughout the club and culminated in the 1988 and 1991 cup titles. The spin-off for England was that Harlequins provided the backbone of their Grand Slam teams in 1991 and 1992.

Above: Pilkington Cup Semi-final, 4 April 1992. Harlequins 15, Leicester 9. Forwards do all the hard work, backs get all the glory; David Pears scores the game's only try for Harlequins.
Right: In the same game, Mick Skinner being devoured by a pack of tigers.
Opposite page: Wavell Wakefield, father of modern forward play, models the mother of all scrum caps, circa 1920.

FACING FORWARDS

No 4: Neil Edwards

Position: Lock **Age:** 28 **Ht:** 6'4½" **Wt:** 18st

If you like your second-rows to be lean, mean and handsome then steer clear of this guy. 'Proud McEdwards' is from the old school of locks: dumpy, cuddly and cauliflower-eared. Just in case you were thinking of throwing away your beer gut and scrum-cap, it's worth noting that these qualities are making a comeback. Last season the Surrey-born lock won his first cap for Scotland, hence the nickname. He fitted so well into the side that by the end of the championship he was the perfect team man: he had developed a rough Scottish burr and, despite having lived south of the border all his life, was avowing his contempt for all Englishmen. Despite all this, 'Eddie' is one of the most popular players on the circuit, a nice guy who was just born the wrong shape and so fell into a nasty trade.

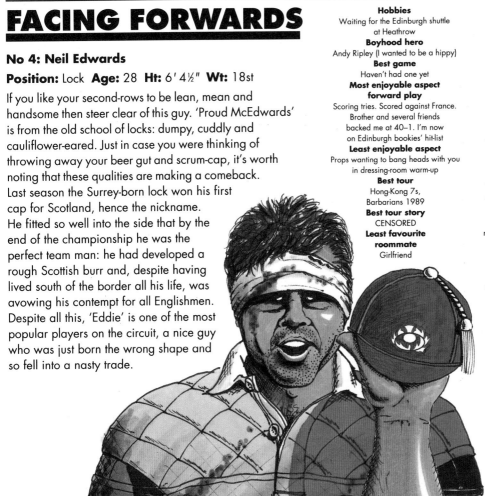

Hobbies
Waiting for the Edinburgh shuttle at Heathrow
Boyhood hero
Andy Ripley (I wanted to be a hippy)
Best game
Haven't had one yet
Most enjoyable aspect forward play
Scoring tries. Scored against France. Brother and several friends backed me at 40–1. I'm now on Edinburgh bookies' hit-list
Least enjoyable aspect
Props wanting to bang heads with you in dressing-room warm-up
Best tour
Hong-Kong 7s, Barbarians 1989
Best tour story
CENSORED
Least favourite roommate
Girlfriend

Favourite drink
Alcohol
Favourite food
Pasta
Favourite film
The Graduate (usual fantasies about older women)
Favourite newspaper
The Independent
Drinking capacity
A lot
Champion drinker in side
Jason Leonard – he may be young but he has a bottomless gut. Has life shares in The Sun, Richmond
Main complaint about game
Too much back-biting.
(Eddie is a founding member of The Bitter and Twisted Club, a London-based gathering of players who feel hard done by. That is, they've usually not been picked for some team or other. Meetings are conducted over champagne breakfasts at the Savoy. Eddie's selection for Scotland caused uproar in the club. Calls for his expulsion were only just resisted but he was demoted to a country member)
Most interesting thing about myself
Wondering how I can keep such a physique on the move for 80 minutes
Who I would most liked to have been
A sly fox because it always leads to a bushy tail

Leicester wear big letters on their backs (and forwards) instead of numbers, so here is a question: what is spelt out if the Leicester hooker, loose-head prop, left lock, inside centre, right lock and right wing line up in a row?

Can you read it without any help from your mum and dad?

ICESTER

Where the hell are they?

Leicester spell trouble at Welford Road, Leicester. Tel: 0533 541607.

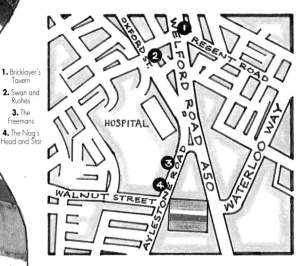

1. Bricklayer's Tavern
2. Swan and Rushes
3. The Freemans
4. The Nag's Head and Star

Where's the bar?

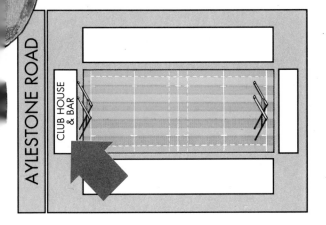

Who scores all the points?
(Shoot that tiger)

Leading scorers in the League 1991/92
J. Liley (3 tries, 19 cons, 25 pens) 125
R. Underwood (9 tries) 36 , J. Harris (1 try, 4 dg) 16, S. Hackney (4 tries) 16, T. Underwood (3 tries) 12
Leicester's 262 League points included 33 tries.

How did they do last year?

PLAYED 12 • WON 6 • DRAWN 1 • LOST 5
Points for: 262 • Points against: 216
6TH IN COURAGE LEAGUE ONE

Where are the nearest pubs?
See the map.

What else?

Founded 1880.
Nickname: 'Tigers'
Second XV: Leicester Ex.1st.

CHANGE STRIP

League History: First Division since 1987.
League Honours: First Division Champions 1988.
Cup Honours: *Winners* 1979, 1980, 1981. *Finalists* 1978, 1983, 1989.

Keen youths were playing rugby in Leicester as early as 1869, but it was the association of three of the city's junior teams in 1880 that marked the foundation of the now famous Tigers, a nickname that originally alluded to the club's striped jerseys. In its first season 13 of the 15 matches played were won and the opponents included the other members of the Midlands' rugby trinity, Northampton and Coventry.

The first games at Welford Road were played in September 1892 but it was the election of Tom Crumbie as secretary three years later that signalled the beginning of a period of steady growth both on and off the field. During his well-spent 33 years in office he never missed a Leicester match. Between 1898 and 1904, the club were unbeaten in the Midland Counties Cup (they actually withdrew thereafter

to allow another team to taste honours) and in 1903 John Miles started a trickle of Leicester players into the England XV. Crumbie was a man of vision. Not content to limit his domain to team building, he set about developing Welford Road into a stadium fit to stage internationals, thereby increasing revenue for the club and guaranteeing financial stability.

In the early 1920s, when the club regularly played 45 matches a season, there was an interesting tactical experiment with a five-threequarter formation. Clearly the emphasis was on attack and in the match against Manchester in 1922, Alastair Smallwood created a Leicester record, scoring seven tries. Another club record maker of the era was Harold Day who collected more than 1000 points for the Tigers when penalty goals were extremely rare.

When Leicestershire were invited to join the English county championship in 1920, the Tigers formed the backbone of the county side; and when, just five seasons old, Leicestershire were crowned unbeaten champions,

Leicester: *No team pic this season, so here's one we prepared earlier:*
Back row: J.A. Allen (Honorary Secretary), R.J. Farrands (Honorary Treasurer), B.T.C. Small (President), I. Bates, R. Tebbutt, A. Marriott, T. Smith, A. Gissing, M. Poole, J.M. Wells, S. Povoas, W. Richardson, S. Redfern, D. Matthews (Coach), A. Foster (Coach), J.T. Thomas (Team Secretary). **Seated:** T. Buttimore, J. Harris, A. Kardooni, S. Kenney, T. Underwood, D. Richards (Captain), L. Cusworth (now retired), B.J. Evans, I.R. Smith, R. Underwood. **Front row:** G. Gerald, J. Liley.

the county trusted to a team comprising entirely Leicester players adopting the club's five-threequarter system.

Between the wars, international players from each of the Home Unions appeared in the unusual lettered jerseys of the club, with George Beamish (Ireland), Wavell Wakefield, Doug Kendrew and Bernard Gadney (England) captaining their countries. When Gadney was in charge of England's most famous win against an overseas side – 13–0 over the 1936 All Blacks – he was helped by three Leicester regulars including Prince Alex Obolensky whose celebrated tries mesmerised the New Zealanders.

Two of the most colourful post-war internationals were Phil Horrocks-Taylor and Tony O'Reilly. The latter tells a wonderful tale of how an Irish colleague was baffled by the former in a big match: 'Horrocks went one way,' related O'Reilly's compatriot, 'Taylor went the other, leaving me holding the hyphen.'

Since the inaugural RFU Cup season (1971–72), the Tigers have been pre-eminent in competition rugby. Coached by Chalky White, Leicester won the cup three years running, thanks to an expansive approach supported by Dusty Hare's deadly kicking. Dusty, whose 4507 points are a club record, was one of seven Leicester caps under the captaincy of Tigers' Peter Wheeler in England's team against Ireland in 1984, and helped the club to win the first Courage League Championship in 1987–8.

Above: 'Ello, 'ello, 'ello: P.C. Dean Richards arrests the ball and proceeds in a northerly direction. And the older you get, the younger he looks.
Above left: Three cups in a row: Leicester 15, Moseley 12; Leicester 21, London Irish 9; Leicester 22, Newcastle Gosforth 15.
Left: Prince Alex Obolensky, circa 1936 – tragically a mere winger.
Opposite page: B.C. Gadney – that rare phenomenon, a captain of an England team that beat the All Blacks.

FACING FORWARDS

No 5: Neil Back

Position: Flanker **Age:** 23 **Ht:** 5' 10" **Wt:** 13½ st

Neil Back has the perfect attribute for a flanker – distinctive hair. Never mind that he stands out because he's shorter than the norm; never mind that he stands out because he's quicker and more involved than the norm; no, what really gets this man noticed is his blond swept-back hair. Think of all the great flankers of recent times: Jean-Pierre Rives, Fergus Slattery, John Taylor and Peter Winterbottom. And they all had that classic flanker's mop of hair – either blond or curly. Ideally of course you'll combine both, and really guarantee yourself a place in the limelight. Did I hear that prop forward at the back say that he always knew flankers were poseurs anyway? Nonsense.

Previous clubs
Nottingham
Hero
Jean-Pierre Rives
Hobbies
Squash, badminton, weight-training
Best match ever played
Barbarians v England 1990
Worst match ever played
Had never had a bad memory
of rugby until...
Middlesex Sevens 1992.
We were hammered by
34 points by London Scottish.
Humiliating

Best opposition forward
Wayne Shelford
Most enjoyable aspect
Scoring tries
Least enjoyable
Big, hairy front five forwards
keeping hands on the ball
Best tour
England B to New Zealand 1992.
And I've not even been on it yet
Best tour story
CENSORED
Most embarrassing moment
There were thousands of them really.
All the way through the
14 minutes of the London Scottish
game in the Middlesex Sevens
Biggest insult
Told that I'm good enough
but not big enough
Favourite drink
Guinness
Favourite food
Pasta
Favourite film
Any Clint Eastwood
Drinking capacity
Not much
Champion drinker in side
Deano
Motto
If you're good enough,
you're big enough

LOND

L ondon Irishmen are usually very lucky – due to the fact that yer men always carry four-leaf clovers with them at The Avenue. This means that *you'll* be lucky if you come away with a win. So how *do* you go about impressing them? Easy! Just go into their club-house and sink ten pints of Guinness. Then you'll be emerald green too!

ON IRISH

Where the hell are they?

London Irish jig about at The Avenue, Sunbury-on-Thames, Middlesex TW16 5EQ. Telephone: 0932 783034.

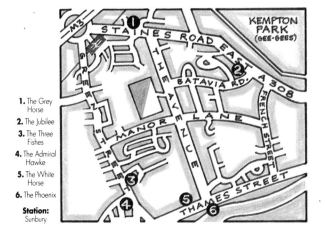

1. The Grey Horse
2. The Jubilee
3. The Three Fishes
4. The Admiral Hawke
5. The White Horse
6. The Phoenix

Station: Sunbury

Where's the bar?

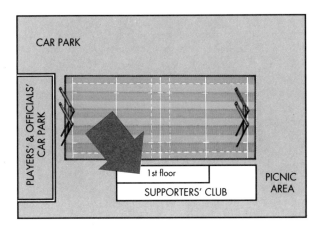

Who scores all the points?
(Make sure their luck runs out)

Leading scorers in the League 1991/92
M. Corcoran (4 tries, 5 cons, 15 pens) 71
B. Mullen (1 try, 3 cons, 10 pens, 2 dg) 46
J. Staples (2 tries) 8, R. Hennessey (2 tries) 8
London Irish's 147 League points included 11 tries.

How did they do last year?

PLAYED 12 • WON 3 • DRAWN 3 • LOST 6
Points for: 147 • Points against: 237
9TH IN COURAGE LEAGUE ONE

Where are the nearest pubs?
See the map.

What else?

Founded 1898.
Nickname: 'The Irish.'
Second XV: Wild Geese.

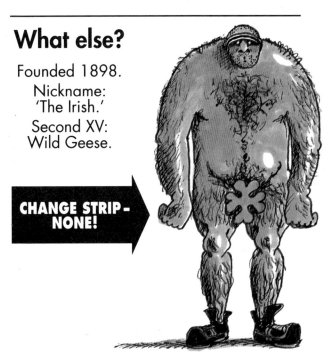

CHANGE STRIP – NONE!

League History: First Division since 1991; Second Division 1987–91.

Cup Honours: *Finalists* 1980.

London Irish were the last of the three big exiles clubs formed in London. The inspiration behind the foundation in 1898 was R.S.V. Dyas, the first captain, though it was the arrival in London of Louis Magee, a noted Irish international, that gave the club the boost needed to establish the Irish at the turn of the century.

Early matches were played at Herne Hill but the rapid expansion of the club compelled the comittee to search for grander quarters. In common with their local rivals they had to tramp the London area for accommodation. Temporary sites were occupied at Stamford Bridge, Wandsworth Common, Walthamstow, Catford, Norbiton and Motspur Park before the exiles settled at Sunbury. The formal opening of the ground was in 1931–32 when Dr W.R.F. Collis, the ex-international forward, was captain of the club.

More doctors have played for London Irish than for any other first-class rugby club. One medic who was one of the most gifted all-round sportsmen to play in the emerald green of the club after the last war was Dr Kevin O'Flanagan. He played rugby for London Irish and soccer for Arsenal on alternate weeks, and in 1947 he was capped for Ireland at both games.

Growing membership prompted moves to establish more extensive facilities at Sunbury in the late '40s, when the senior XVs were forced to share premises at the Rectory Field with Blackheath to enable the flourishing junior sections of London Irish to continue playing at Sunbury.

Jim Corcoran, John Daly, Tom Gavin and Des O'Brien were London Irish's representatives in the successful Ireland Triple Crown-winning teams of 1948

London Irish, 1991–92: Back row: M. Leonard, S. Geoghegan, B. Mullen, M. Egan, A. Higgins, C. Buss, T. Clancy, P. Collins, D. Pegler, J. Keohane.
Front row: J. Byrne, D. Curtis, P. Young, J. Staples (Captain), W. Kearns, G. Halpin, J. McFarland.

and 1949. In the following decade several British Lions were supplied by the club, including Robin Thompson, captain of the 1955 Lions in South Africa.

The 1959–60 season was note-worthy. 'Fitzy's Bar', the spacious club house, was opened and the exiles enjoyed the best playing season of their history. 'It was unquestionably a first-class team who played open football with an excellent pack of forwards, admirably supported by the backs,' the *Playfair Rugby Annual* concluded on a season in which 30 matches were won and three drawn. Internationals Andy Mulligan and Sean McDermott, the half-backs, were the side's tacticians, Ronnie McCarten on the wing played for Ireland the next season and many of the fifteen appeared in Irish trials.

Retirements and career moves precipitated the disintegration of the class of '61 and the club was cast into rugby obscurity until John Moroney and Ollie Waldron helped to raise playing standards during the late '60s.

London Irish have always relied on former players to steer the club's development. Post-war stalwarts Michael O'Connor, Ron Johnston and Dr Pat Parfrey were

president, secretary and coach respectively in 1980 when the Irish became only the second London club to reach the RFU Cup final. A side led by Dr John O'Driscoll lost 21–9 to Leicester Tigers, despite scoring the only try of the match.

Another former player, Kevin Short, made a big impact when he coached the side in 1990. Demanding commitment from the entire club, he imbued the exiles with confidence. Four backs were capped by Ireland and the culmination of his work was promotion to Division One of the Courage Leagues.

Above: *Northampton v London Irish, Courage League 23rd November 1991. A Saint helps Jim Staples ascend to heaven.*
Above left: *In the same match, John Byrne wants to kick, Simon Geoghegan wants to run. Who says it's just forwards who can't make decisions?*
Opposite: *Louis Magee, the man without whom London Irish would just be a twinkle in R.S.V. Dyas' Irish eye.*

FACING FORWARDS

No 6: Paul Collins

Position: Flanker **Age:** 32 **Ht:** 6'3" **Wt:** 15½ st

He's quiet, studious, industrious and perfectly mannered. Could this just be a front for when the lights go out on the pitch and come on in the bar at Sunbury? Lurking behind that urbane, placid exterior might there just not be one of those Moss Keane Irishmen who drink, swear, fight and then embrace you in one huge emotional bear hug? Paul Collins says not. But just wait until you try and take that measly, insignif-icant oval-shaped, white leather thing from him and see how the rage begins to swell in his breast, the fire steam from his nostrils and the anger flash in his eyes. Then does yer man show his true colours – playing the game with typical green-shirted vigour.

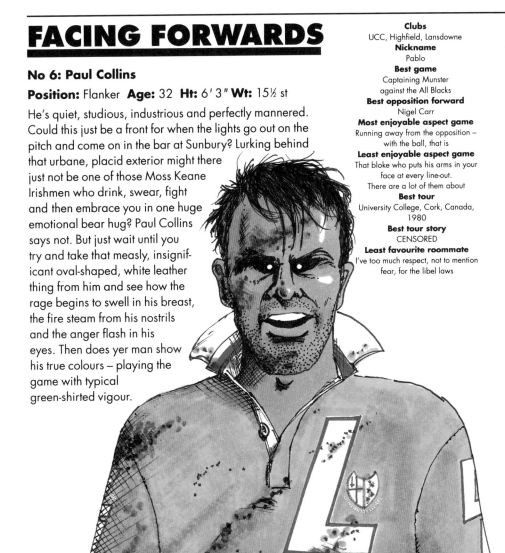

Clubs
UCC, Highfield, Lansdowne
Nickname
Pablo
Best game
Captaining Munster
against the All Blacks
Best opposition forward
Nigel Carr
Most enjoyable aspect game
Running away from the opposition –
with the ball, that is
Least enjoyable aspect game
That bloke who puts his arms in your
face at every line-out.
There are a lot of them about
Best tour
University College, Cork, Canada,
1980
Best tour story
CENSORED
Least favourite roommate
I've too much respect, not to mention
fear, for the libel laws

Most embarrassing moment
Playing for Munster
with a pair of rogue shorts which kept
dropping round my ankles
Favourite drink
Foster's
Favourite food
A good steak
Favourite film
Dead Men Don't Wear Plaid
Favourite newspaper
Daily Telegraph
Motto
Bereidh (be prepared)
Drinking capacity
Ever diminishing
Champion drinker
Aidan Higgins
Biggest compliment ever paid
Being selected for Ireland
Biggest insult ever received
Being dropped by Ireland
after one game
**Who I would most liked
to have been**
Charlie Haughey

LONDO

London Scottish F.C. live down by the River MacThames in MacRichmond. They are the team that made jock straps famous. The model illustrated is the 'Cameron' – a great favourite at Kew Foot Road. If you haven't heard of a jock strap before, make sure you get one now. And remember: you should always pull on a jock strap before you take on those strapping jocks.

Where the hell are they?

Jocky for position at Richmond Athletic Ground, Kew Foot Road, Richmond, Surrey TW9 2SS. Telephone: 081-940 0379.

1. The Blue Anchor
2. The Shaftesbury Arms
3. The Hope of Richmond
4. The Triple Crown
5. The Orange Tree
6. The Duke of York
7. Bull and Bush
8. The Jock Strap (only joking!)

Station: Richmond

Where's the bar?

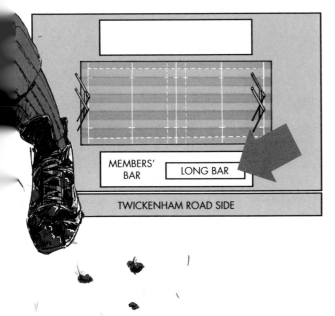

MEMBERS' BAR   LONG BAR

TWICKENHAM ROAD SIDE

Who scores all the points?
(Up and under the kilt with this lot)

Leading scorers in the League 1991/92

N. Grecian (11 tries, 13 cons, 17 pens) 121
M. Appleson (2 tries, 9 cons, 6 pens, 1dg) 47, D. White (6 tries) 24,
I. Morrison (3 tries, 1 con) 14
London Scottish's 304 League points included 45 tries.

How did they do last year?

PLAYED 12 • WON 11 • DRAWN 0 • LOST 1
Points for: 304 • Points against: 130
WINNERS COURAGE LEAGUE TWO

Where are the nearest pubs?
See the map.

What else?

Founded 1878.
Nickname: 'The Scottish.'
Second XV: London Scottish Ex. 1st.

CHANGE STRIP

League History: Second Division 1987–89, 1990–92; Third Division 1989–90.
League Honours: Third Division Champions 1990.
Cup Honours: Finalists 1974.

The oldest of the London exile clubs, the Scottish were formed on 10th April 1878. Writing of the early years, former player R.H. Hedderwick recalled 'the preliminary and most burning question to have been that of the ground upon which to play our matches. During the summer of 1878 the committee scoured the environs of London with great ardour, but with so little success that the club had to open its career on an odd corner of Blackheath Common.'

After brief spells playing at Clapham, Lee and Hampstead, London Scottish settled at Old Deer Park in 1888 before moving across the park to begin its joint tenancy with Richmond six years later. Recruiting students from Oxford and Cambridge, the exiles became a potent playing force in the 1880s and 1890s, a period in which the influence of two Scottish internationals, Bill Maclagan and George Lindsay, was significant.

Maclagan was already an established international when he joined a London stockbroking firm in 1880. As player, captain and later, president, his footballing skills, intellectual energy and powers of persuasion during the following four decades firmly placed London Scottish in the top rank. Lindsay, who was a journalist with numerous connections, complemented Maclagan's work by ensuring that the club received its fair share of good publicity. For many years Maclagan held the Scottish cap record while Lindsay's feat of scoring five tries for Scotland against Wales remains to this day the longest surviving individual record in international rugby.

The heyday of the club was in the first decade of the century. In 1906–07, when Scotland beat the visiting Springboks and won the Triple Crown, two-thirds of the national side were London Scottish members. The following season 14 exiles were capped.

Tragic losses were suffered in the Great War. Of the sixty men fielded in the club's four fifteens on the last Saturday of the 1913–14 season, only four survived the

London Scottish, 1991–92: Back row: A. McHarg (Coach), A. Cushing (Coach), D. Glles (Physiotherapist), J. Baird, C. Bannerman, B. Hillicks, D. Signorini, R. Scott, D. Cronin, B. McKay, P. Burnell, M. SLy, A. Campbell, N. Provan, F. Harrold, S. Chamberlain (Physiotherapist), R. Luke (Club Secretary)
Front row: J. Beddow, I. McLeod, C. Russell, N. Grecian, S. McDonald, L. Renwick, D. Millard, R. Cramb (Captain), A.C.W. Boyle (President), I. Dixon, M. Appleson, K. Troup, G. Corbett, A. Withers-Green, J. Beasley, A. Cruikshank, I. Morrison.

hostilities unscathed. More than 200 members enlisted. Altogether the club's losses numbered 69 killed, with 52 wounded. So it was a tribute to the organisational skills of the exiles' secretary Colonel 'Duggie' Lyall Grant, that London Scottish were able to muster six fifteens soon after the war.

It was not until forty years later however that sustained playing success gave considerable satisfaction to the club. There began in 1960 a remarkable domination of the Middlesex Sevens. London Scottish appeared in six consecutive finals, won five, and two of their numerous internationals, Iain Laughland and Jim Shackleton, had the distinction of playing in all six. 1964–65 was hailed as the best season in the club's history. Under lock Frans ten Bos only three matches of the thirty played were lost.

Another respected Scottish lock, Alistair McHarg, has served the club admirably for the past 24 years. The exiles' most-capped player, he was a member of the side that reached the RFU cup final in 1974 and masterminded the recent rise from Third to First Division of the Courage Leagues. For his dedication to the club he was awarded a special London Scottish cap – an honour he shares with Dr. Doug Smith, the London Scot who managed the 1971 British Lions.

Above: *Haggises fly higher than Wasps – the proof. Rob Scott catches a line-out ball, supported by Doug Signorini's fork-lift (hidden), Alistair Cruikshank and Bim Mackay.*
Above left: *Old London Scottish programme – 6 February 1937, the Jocks mauled The Tigers 16–0.*
Opposite page: *London Scottish knocked seven kinds of s**t out of their opponents in the Middlesex Sevens Finals in the early '60s. The programme for the first of their five wins, in 1960: London Scottish 16, London Welsh 5.*

FACING FORWARDS

No 7: Derek White

Position: N°8 **Age:** 34 **Ht:** 6'4" **Wt:** 16st 4lbs

Last season Derek White retired from international rugby. If the image of an old man in his bathchair, rug tucked around his knees and slippers warming by the fire, is the one that comes to mind, then you're in for a bit of a shock.

The Big Scot is still breathing fire. The quieter man of that famed Scottish back-row of Calder, White, Jeffrey, he did his talking on the field. The most-capped Scottish N°8 and the joint record-holder for the number of tries for a Scottish forward, Derek White still has a bit of damage to inflict at the Athletic Ground this season.

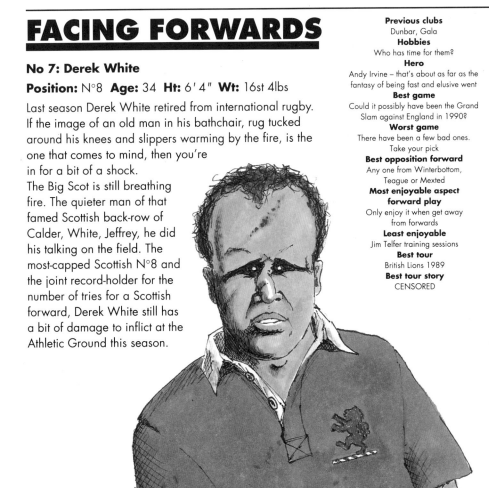

Previous clubs
Dunbar, Gala
Hobbies
Who has time for them?
Hero
Andy Irvine – that's about as far as the fantasy of being fast and elusive went
Best game
Could it possibly have been the Grand Slam against England in 1990?
Worst game
There have been a few bad ones. Take your pick
Best opposition forward
Any one from Winterbottom, Teague or Mexted
Most enjoyable aspect forward play
Only enjoy it when get away from forwards
Least enjoyable
Jim Telfer training sessions
Best tour
British Lions 1989
Best tour story
CENSORED

Least favourite roommate
Scott Hastings
(makes only marginally less noise than when awake)
Most embarrassing moment
Against England.
Aimed punch at Probyn; hit Jeffrey all right. Our Jeffrey that is
Favourite drink
The Balvenie
Favourite food
Lasagne
Favourite film
'Casablanca'
Favourite paper
Daily Telegraph
Drinking capacity
Limited
Champion drinker
Del Boy Cronin
Biggest compliment ever paid
Someone once thought I was John Jeffrey
Biggest insult ever received
Someone once thought I was John Jeffrey

NORT

Northampton – home of the 'Saints.' Do you know what a saint is? Well, a typical saint is devout, godly and full of virtue. Nothing like any of the Northampton players... in fact, devils are much more common at the Saints' ground. So next time you travel down to Northampton, you had better be a very good boy the night before you play, and make sure that you say all of your prayers, bless you.

Where the hell are they?

Northampton perform miracles at Franklin's Gardens, Weedon Road, Northampton. Telephone: 0604 751543.

1. The Red Rover
2. Thomas A Becket
3. Foundry Arms

Station: Northampton

Where's the bar?

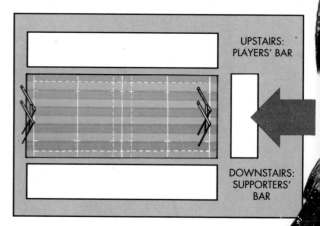

UPSTAIRS: PLAYERS' BAR

DOWNSTAIRS: SUPPORTERS' BAR

IAMPTON

Who scores all the points?
(Damn them.)

Leading scorers in the League 1991/92

J. Steele (10 cons, 28 pens, 2 dg) 110
H. Thorneycroft (5 tries) 20
I. Hunter (4 tries, 1 dg) 19,
M. Dawson (1 try, 1 con, 2 pens) 12
Northampton's 209 League points
included 22 tries.

Last year's record

PLAYED 12 • W9 • D1 • L2
Points for: 209 • Against: 136
3RD IN COURAGE LEAGUE 1

Nearest pubs?
See the map.

What else?

Founded 1880.
Nickname:
'Saints.'
Second XV:
Wanderers.

CHANGE STRIP →

League History: First Division since 1990;
Second Division 1987–90.
League Honours: Second Division Champions 1990.
Cup Honours: Finalists 1991.

When the Rev. Wathen Wigg, a young curate at St. James's Church in Northampton, founded a rugby club at the church in 1878, he had no idea that the 'Saints' would march on to occupy a place in the higher ranks of English club rugby.

In 1880, the church lads amalgamated with the Unity club to form Northampton RFC. The new club soon established fixtures with Leicester and in 1891 moved to Franklin's Gardens, still in the parish of St. James's.

The remarkable Kingston family provided the backbone of the club in the 1890s. Eight of the family turned out for the 'Saints' and Tim Kingston appeared at scrum-half in an England trial in 1900, while his brother,

W.H. Kingston, scored over 200 tries for the club.

Harry Weston, a tough, uncompromising forward who farmed at Yardley Gobion, was Northampton's first international player. He won his only England cap against Scotland in 1901, but saw his son Billy pack down for Northampton and England in the 1930s.

The player credited with transforming the 'Saints' into a first-class club was the legendary Edgar Mobbs, a powerful threequarter who ran with an unusual knee-high action. During his captaincy (1907–08 to 1912–13) the record of the club was one of the best in Britain. When Northampton celebrated its golden jubilee in 1930, the club's historians conferred on Mobbs the title of greatest figure in the history of the 'Saints.' Mobbs died a hero's death in the Great War, but his memory is annually revered at the East Midlands–Barbarians fixture, traditionally staged at Northampton.

Northampton 1991–92: Back row: J. Griffiths, R. Tebbutt, G. Pearce, C. Allen, M. Ord, R. Nancekivell. **Middle row:** G. Ross (Chief Coach), R. Horwood (Secretary), P. Roworth, G. Baldwin, W. Shelford, S. Foale, I. Hunter, D. Elkington, P. Whiting (Physiotherapist), B. Corless (Director of Coaching), B. Ingram (Team Secretary). **Front row:** B. Taylor, B. Ward, P. Pask, J. Olver (Captain), R. Slinn (President), H. Thorneycroft, F. Packman, R. McNaughton, M. Dawson.

The club has had its fair share of practical jokers. A favourite wheeze of the team in their heyday under Mobbs was to masquerade as train ticket collectors on away-day visits to Wales. Players waited for the fireworks to start when the official collector made his round. Only a captain with Mobbs's charm could leave victims laughing as he intervened to explain the prank.

Northampton took pride in their forwards between the wars. Ray Longland, a Toby jug prop, was an indestructible force for club and country for many years. Indeed, had not war interrupted his career in 1939, he would have become England's longest-serving international – a record held, incidentally, by the current Northampton prop, Gary Pearce. Another popular scrummaging 'Saint' was John Dicks, a local farmer who appeared with Longland and Billy Weston in England's Triple Crown-winning pack of 1934.

From 1947 to the early '60s, Northampton vied with their Midland rivals, Coventry and Leicester, for the unofficial title of English club champions. Don White led a talented side which included a clutch of outstanding players: Lewis Cannell, Jeff Butterfield and Dickie Jeeps in the backs; Ron Jacobs, Phil Taylor

and Don White himself in the pack. The 'Saints' had a representative in every England international team between 1951 and 1962, and won more than three quarters of their club matches in the second half of the period.

Now, after a recent period of relative decline, the arrival and expertise of Wayne Shelford and the consolidation under John Olver have returned Northampton to the top flight of English rugby.

Above: *The 1991 Pilkington Cup Final, Northampton v Harlequins. Here, Tim Rodber is about to viciously attack Peter Winterbottom's clenched fist with his nose.*
Left: *A holy trinity of 'Saints': Harry Weston, Ray Longland and John Dicks.*

FACING FORWARDS

No 8: John Olver

Position: Hooker **Age:** 30 **Ht:** 5' 9" **Wt:** 13½ st

Avoid this man at all costs if you end up anywhere near the England squad. Don't even be disarmed if he is not actually carrying a bucket of water for, pound to a penny, one Mickey Skinner will be lurking round a corner somewhere ready to douse Olver. The pair have had a running competition for years now to see who can catch the other one out. Olver leads by a short head which in fact also neatly sums up the way he plays his rugby. Not the biggest but certainly one of the most competitive men in the game. John had almost given up picking the splinters from his backside after sitting on the replacement bench for so long when he was finally rewarded with his first cap, against Argentina, two years ago.

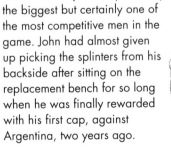

Clubs
Harlequins (1981–90)
Hobbies
Shooting, fishing, golf
Heroes
Fran Cotton, even though I knew I would never be his size
Best game
Cup final 1988, 'Quins v Bristol
Worst game
Hundreds of them
Best opposition forward
Richard Loe, who was certainly the most menacing;
Peter Winterbottom, who opposed me in house matches at Rossall.
He's been an easier touch since
Most enjoyable aspect forward play
Scoring tries and I've certainly got enough fingers with which to count them
Most embarrassing moment
Caught by TV arguing with Fred Howard in Cup match with Bath.
Stuart Barnes had moved the ball a couple of metres nearer, which I pointed out to Fred.
Stuart kicked the goal, then another from halfway immediately afterwards awarded against me for arguing.
The 50 pupils watching from my school were most impressed.

Best tour
Middlesex to Canada, 1983
Best tour story
CENSORED.
Least favourite roommate
Ollie Redman, with whom I shared for six weeks in the World Cup.
He's far too tidy and organised
Relationship with referees
Sumptuous
Ambitions
To avoid getting another bucket of water on my head
Favourite drink
Bitter
Favourite food
Chicken
Drinking capacity
Small
Champion drinker in side
Gary Pearce – he's had enough years to practise
Motto
Get your retaliation in first
Biggest compliment ever paid
Being selected for England
Biggest insult
I go suddenly deaf
Most interesting thing about myself
I've been voted the world's most boring man for the last five years by the England squad

Orrell... smoke, grit and tears. A match against Orrell is not fun. If you want to know what it *is* like, get your Big Brother to read you both 'The Road to Wigan Pier' and 'Scrum Down and Out in Paris and London.' Being sent to bed early without your beer and crisps is nothing compared to a ruck or a maul at Edgehall Road.

ORRELL

Where the hell are they?

In a lay-by off the M6 called
Edgehall Road, Orrell, near Wigan.
Telephone: 0695 623193.

1. Orrell Post
2. Owl Inn
3. Abbey Lakes
4. Rose and Crown
5. Delph Tavern
6. Sandbrook
7. Robin Hood
8. Station Hotel

Station: Orrell

Where's the bar?

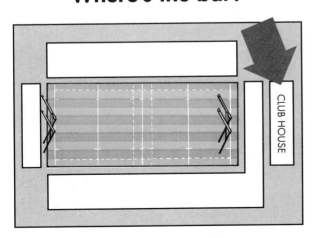

Who scores all the points?

(Deal with these Orrells or else.)

Leading scorers in the League 1991/92
M. Strett (1 try, 8 cons, 26 pens, 2 dg) 104
D. Morris (7 tries) 28
N. Heslop (6 tries) 24, P. Halsall (3 tries) 12
Orrell's 204 League points
included 26 tries.

How did they do last year?

PLAYED 12 • WON 10 • DRAWN 0 • LOST 2
Points for: 204 • Points against: 95
2ND IN COURAGE LEAGUE ONE

Where are the nearest pubs?

See the map.

What else?

Founded 1927.
Nickname:
'Little Ommers.'
Second XV:
The Second XV.

CHANGE STRIPS

45

League History: First Division since 1987.

Orrell were founded in 1927, making the club the youngest of the current members of Division One of the Courage Leagues. Forced to lead a frugal existence in the depressed '30s, there is a story (possibly apocryphal) that when club officials reassembled after the Second World War, only fifty pence remained in the coffers. So the intrepid committee immediately blew the lot on a round of drinks.

Orrell have never looked back since. The club has pursued a policy of sensible forward-planning and their ground and facilities at Edgehall Road are now numbered among the best in the country. One of the most novel fund-raising ideas – the popular Whitsun club carnival – became a money-spinner enabling more than £20,000 worth of improvements to be made at the ground during the '60s.

Improvements in playing standards have gone hand in hand with progress off the field. A watershed in the club's history was reached under Bill Huxley's effective leadership in 1964. The first XV beat Fylde, then one of the top sides in the north of England, Eric Lyon became Orrell's first England trialist, appearing for the Whites at Weston-super-Mare, and the club lost only two of its matches.

The upshot of these successes was an improved fixture list. Regular meetings with better clubs in turn led to the rapid enhancement of the club's profile and in 1972–73, the second season of the RFU club competition, the focus of

Orrell 1990–91: Back row: S. Booth (Physiotherapist), D. Seabrook (Director of Coaching), I. Wynn, P. Halsall, S. Bibby, C. Cusani, B. Kimmins, C. Brierley, N. Ashurst, D. Cleary, P. Manley, M. Glynn, P. Moss (Assistant Coach), S. Lanford.
Middle row: G. Ainscough Snr. (1st XV Touch Judge), P. Cusack (now with Cockermouth), D. Morris, S. Taberner (Captain), R. Pimblett (Club Chairman) D. Southern, B. Taberner (Retiring President), G. Ainscough Jnr. (now with Leicester Tigers), N. Hitchen, M. Strett, B. Lyon (Club Coach).
Front row: C. O'Toole (now with Liverpool St Helens), A. Marshall, S. Hayter, M. Hynes.

national attention was on Orrell when they went out to Coventry in the quarter-final of the cup.

The same season, Frank Anderson became the first international capped from the club when he played for England against the All Blacks. Anderson was one of four Orrell players in the Lancashire side who won the County Championship, and Des Seabrook, the club's number eight, captained the county.

Seabrook was captain again the following season. The club had another successful RFU cup run, reaching the semi-finals, and induced one of the best one-liners about Orrell after Harlequins were knocked out in the second round: 'We were beaten by a lay-by off the M6,' quipped the losers' captain.

In October 1977, Orrell staged an England Under-23 international against France. Their young right wing, John Carleton, made his representative debut in that game. He went on to play for England, became the club's first British Lion (1980) and is Orrell's most-capped player.

Consistent performances by an attractive side committed to 15-man rugby enabled Orrell to finish at or near the top of the Northern Merit tables in the early 1980s. In the quest for excellence the club continued to strengthen its fixture list and, in 1984–85, created a remarkable English

club record when Sammy Southern's team amassed 1295 points.

Seabrook's forceful influence as chairman has been a significant factor in the most successful spell in Orrell's history. He took them to promotion from table B of the primitive Rugby Football Union merit leagues and the team has become firmly established in the First Division of the Courage Leagues proper, finishing second to Bath on points difference in last April's hectic climax to the title race.

Above: Orrell 16, Gloucester 25; Pilkington Cup quarter final, 22 February 1992. Dewi Morris spins out a monster pass which eventually landed over half a mile away on the M6 – causing long tailbacks and diversions on the southbound carriageway.
Opposite: The last game of the season – Nottingham go down and Orrell are pipped at the winning post by Bath.

FACING FORWARDS

No 9: Sammy Southern

Position: Prop **Age:** 39 **Ht:** 5' 10" **Wt:** 15½ st

Does anyone call this man by his real name – David Southern? If you thought Wigan Pier was something of a historical landmark around these parts then you've obviously never visited Edgehall Road. Sammy Southern is such an ancient and distinguished part of the local heritage that he is soon to be sponsored by the National Trust. He first played for the club when he was 15 years old, having taught William Webb Ellis everything he knew at school. He is a founding member of the front-row union, who were a great inspiration to the Tolpuddle Martyrs. Sammy has captained the club with great distinction and, from December, will be living proof that life begins at 40.

First club
Roman Invaders RFC (25 BC – 43 AD)
Hobbies
Trying to find out what a rugby ball looks like. You don't see too much of it in the front-row
Worst game
Aargh! Don't remind me. I wake sweating and screaming every night, seeing that last second Huw Davies drop goal go between the posts. We lost to Wasps and so lost the championship
Best opposition forward
Charlie Faulkner, Pontypool. It's said that they modelled the Rock of Gibraltar on Charlie. I can see why – nothing can shift him
Best aspect of forward play
Those rare moments of freedom when they let us out of our dark cells and we can romp around the field with the ball. Excuse the fantasy: it gets like that after so many years inside
What I like most about the game
The communal drinking. No matter how many times you've been hit, butted or kicked, there's always time for a shared pint afterwards

Best tour
Zimbabwe with Lancashire, 1990
Best tour story
CENSORED
Motto
Don't quit
Favourite drink
Murphys
Favourite food
Chicken
Favourite film
Never allowed out of front-row to see one
Favourite paper
Whichever one is lying around
Drinking capacity
Up to the neck
Champion drinker in side
Dave Cleary, a publican who knows his business from the inside out
Ambition
To see out the century
Relationship with referees
I've had many stimulating conversations with them although they may not have seen them that way
Biggest compliment ever paid
A Gloucester committee man reckoned that the way I played I must have been born there

Rugby started a long, long time ago at Rugby School. One day a boy called Webb Ellis decided to cheat at football. Picking up the ball, he deflated it so that it was egg-shaped, and ran into the goal to score a 'try.' But the ref gave a free kick and Webb Ellis was taken away and beaten up. So don't forget: if you cheat at Rugby, they'll beat you up too.

'UGBY

Where the hell are they?

Rugby will teach you a lesson at Webb Ellis Road, off Bilton Road, Rugby. Telephone: 0788 542252.

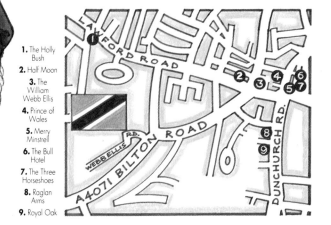

1. The Holly Bush
2. Half Moon
3. The William Webb Ellis
4. Prince of Wales
5. Merry Minstrel
6. The Bull Hotel
7. The Three Horseshoes
8. Raglan Arms
9. Royal Oak

Who scores all the points?
(Tame these Lions)

Leading scorers in the League 1991/92
M. Mapletoft (1 try, 4 cons, 15 pens, 1dg) 60, R. Hensley (4 pens) 12
R. Pell (4 pens) 12, E. Saunders (2 tries) 8
D. Bishop (2 tries) 8
Rugby's 124 League points included 11 tries.

How did they do last year?

PLAYED 12 • WON 2 • DRAWN 3 • LOST 7
Points for: 124 • Points against: 252
11TH IN COURAGE LEAGUE ONE

Where are the nearest pubs?
See the map.

Where's the bar?

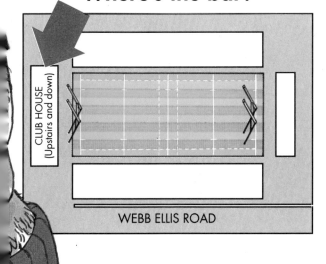

CLUB HOUSE (Upstairs and down)

WEBB ELLIS ROAD

What else?

Founded 1873.
Nickname: 'Lions.'
Second XV: Wanderers.

CHANGE STRIP

League History: First Division since 1991; Second Division 1989–91; Third Division 1988–89; Area League North 1987–88.

League Honours: Area League North Champions 1988. Second Division Champions 1991.

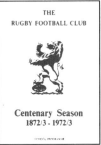

THE
RUGBY FOOTBALL CLUB

Centenary Season
1872/3 - 1972/3

Rugby of course holds a unique place in the early history of the game but it was not until 1873 that a town club was officially formed. The seeds of the foundation were set in the late 1860s when Rugby School masters and Old Rugbeians of Town House met to play informal matches.

Indeed, the white jerseys of the School bearing the lion emblem of the dayboy's house, from which the town club derived their nickname (Lions), were the original uniform adopted by Rugby Football Club. Only recently, Rugby switched to a more colourful garb.

History shows that the 1877–78 team was the most successful of the early club XVs. They won 18 and drew three of their 22 matches. The Midland Counties Cup was won in 1886 and retained in 1887 but a bleak period followed until Lancelot Percival, son of a former Rugby School Head Master, came down from Oxford to lead the side in the 1890s. Capped as a student, Percival, who was a vicar, went on to be the first player capped for England direct from Rugby.

Another English international, Geoff Conway, arrived to teach classics at Rugby School in 1922. His experience was an asset to the town club. Again the Lions' waning fortunes revived and Rugby reached the final of the Midland Counties Cup in 1924. T.L. Thomas led the side the next year when the highlights were wins against Northampton and Coventry

Rugby 1991–92: Back row: D. Manu, J. Baker*, S. Glover, T. Revan, G. Tregilgas, P. Bowman, N. Cooper*, A. Ruddlesdin, E. Saunders.
Front row: D. Watson, S. Vaudin*, J. Aldwinckle, R. Cox, R. Pell, M.R. Ellis, M. Mapletoft, W. Bramble. *These players have since left the club.

as the club improved its fixtures list.

Two popular lock forwards, Norman Marr and Eric Bates, captained Rugby in the following decade. Marr was an England trialist whilst playing at Sunderland and Bates, club skipper in 1938–39, appeared for the Rest XV which beat England 17–3 in the final trial that season. The outbreak of war deprived him of England honours.

Stan Purdy, educated in the town (at Lawrence Sheriff School) and capped direct from Rugby (against Scotland in 1962) was the oustanding club product of post-war years. He captained the Lions between 1958 and 1963 and appeared more than 60 times for Warwickshire during the county's unprecedented run of seven titles in the County Championship (1958–65).

Above: David Bishop dribbles (and salivates) with the ball.
Top: Eric Bates (third from left in the front row), England's unpicked lock.
Right: A leopard can't change its spots, but Lions can change their strips, it seems.
Opposite: One hundred years of Rugby (the game) at Rugby (the place).

Desperate financial straits propelled Rugby into the hands of liquidators in 1986 before a rescue package put together by Mal Malik, who joined the Lions as a flanker, promised a future for the club. England hooker Steve Brain also joined Rugby and there began a golden period in the club's history. From the relative obscurity of Area League North the team's rise to the First Division in just five seasons under coaches Andy Johnson and Allen Foster has been the outstanding success story of the Courage Leagues.

However, the Lions were immersed in problems as they escaped relegation last April. Chairman David Rees' resignation, internal wrangles and unsettled legal action against the club detracted from Rugby's enjoyment of the irrefutable playing advances made recently.

FACING FORWARDS

No 10: Steve Brain

Position: Hooker **Age:** 38 **Ht:** 5' 10½" **Wt:** 16st

You may have met this man before or rather stepped over him one night on your way out of the bar. Brainie is one of the old school – play hard then drink hard. There aren't many left, more's the pity.

The new fitness craze was brought in to try and get rid of players like him.
It didn't work. At the ripe old age of 38 he's still sinking opposition hookers and then sinking pints of Marstons Pedigree in the bar afterwards. A hard man on the field: a soft friendly man off it.

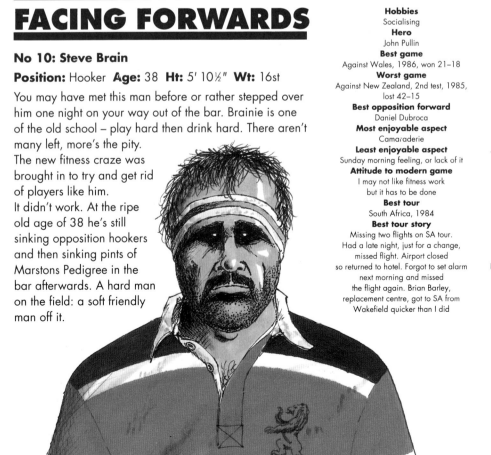

Hobbies
Socialising
Hero
John Pullin
Best game
Against Wales, 1986, won 21–18
Worst game
Against New Zealand, 2nd test, 1985,
lost 42–15
Best opposition forward
Daniel Dubroca
Most enjoyable aspect
Camaraderie
Least enjoyable aspect
Sunday morning feeling, or lack of it
Attitude to modern game
I may not like fitness work
but it has to be done
Best tour
South Africa, 1984
Best tour story
Missing two flights on SA tour.
Had a late night, just for a change,
missed flight. Airport closed
so returned to hotel. Forgot to set alarm
next morning and missed
the flight again. Brian Barley,
replacement centre, got to SA from
Wakefield quicker than I did

Relationship with referees
Mellowed
Ambition
To be manager of England
Favourite drink
Marstons Pedigree
Favourite food
Tomatoes on toast
Favourite film
'Jason and the Argonauts'
Favourite paper
Daily Telegraph
Motto
A man is incomplete until he's married,
then he becomes twisted
Drinking capacity
An anaesthetist asked once if I drank.
I told her my normal intake.
She then gave me enough gas
to knock out a rhinoceros
Champion drinker
At Rugby, yours truly.
But Wade Dooley is the real king
Biggest insult
Brian Moore not turning out against me
8 times in a row
**Most interesting thing
about myself**
My drunken conversation

SAR

Saracens mainly live in Southgate, Cockfosters and up on Winchmore Hill in posh houses. They are called the Saracens after those fierce arabs (not half as fierce as this lot though) that we fought in the Crusades a long time ago. Also, Saracen is the name of a big tank. Forwards like tanks, don't they?

Where the hell are they?

The Saracens crusade at the Bramley Road Sports Ground, Chase Side, Southgate, London N14. Telephone: 081-449 3770.

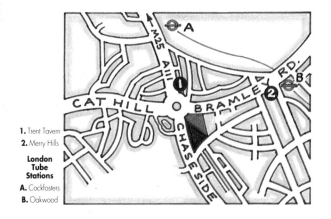

1. Trent Tavern
2. Merry Hills

London Tube Stations
A. Cockfosters
B. Oakwood

Who scores all the points?
(Get these one-eyed sons of camels)

Leading scorers in the League 1991/92
B. Rudling (1 try, 9 cons, 20 pens, 4 dg) 94
M. Gregory (4 tries) 16, A. Lee (2 pens, 2 dg) 12, B. Davies (3 tries) 12
Saracens' 176 League points included 18 tries.

How did they do last year?

PLAYED 12 • WON 7 • DRAWN 1 • LOST 4
Points for: 176 • Points against: 165
5TH IN COURAGE LEAGUE ONE

Where are the nearest pubs?
See the map.

What else?

Founded 1876.
Nickname: 'Sarries.'
Second XV: Crusaders.

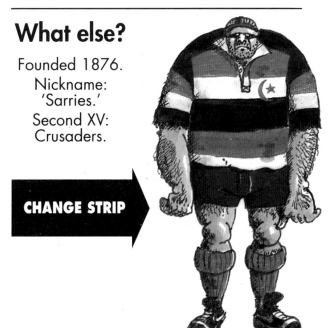

CHANGE STRIP

Where's the bar?

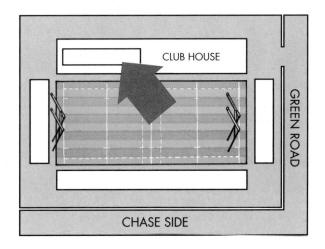

CLUB HOUSE

GREEN ROAD

CHASE SIDE

League History: First Division since 1989.
Second Division 1987–89.

League Honours: Second Division Champions 1989.

The early years of the club resembled those of their London rivals, Wasps and Harlequins. Saracens was a name adopted by a group of former pupils of Marylebone Philological School (later known as St. Marylebone GS) who began playing organised rugby on Primrose Hill in 1876. Great travellers, the club occupied grounds at Clapton, Walthamstow, Tufnell Park, Hornsey and Finchley, amongst others, before settling at Chase Side, Southgate in 1923.

Saracens' membership doubled between 1876 and 1880, helped by an 'unholy' alliance with a neighbouring club named the Crusaders, and in the early 1880s the club boasted an enviable playing record. Led by one Alfred Jenkins, Saracens were unbeaten from 1882 to 1886. Indeed, during the final season of invincibility, the club conceded only one try in 16 games.

Keen to parade their talents on a wider stage, Saracens were the protagonists in the foundation of the Essex County Union in 1885 and supplied nine of the county's first representative team. For more than a century now the Home Counties, principally Middlesex and Hertfordshire, have benefited in the county championship from the expertise of Saracens players. When Middlesex met Lancashire in the county championship final at Twickenham in 1990 there were four Saracens, including the captain Floyd Steadman, in their team.

A feature of the club's teams up to the outbreak of the Great War was the service of the remarkable Bongard family. Three brothers J.L., S.D. and C.S. were in various Saracens teams between 1885 and successive

Saracens 1991–92: Back row: S. Domoni, A. McPherson, B. Rudling, M. Gregory, C. Tarbuck, D. Dooley, G. Clarke, S. Reed, A. Lee.
Middle row: J. Davies (Coach), M. Despy (Team Manager), E. Lewis (Physiotherapist), G. Botterman, B. Crawley, M. Langley, L. Adamson, J. Cassell, S. Nilson, J. Heggadon (President), B. Millar (Chairman of Selectors), A. Thomas (Psychologist).
Front row: M. Evans (Coach), M. Sexton (Physiotherapist), D. Choules, S. Robinson, R. Andrews, J. Buckton (Captain), A. Roda, B. Davies, J. Locke, B. Downes (Touch Judge).

generations of the dynasty have graced the second half of the club's history.

Fielding only one team in 1919 when the club resumed after the war, the playing strength rapidly grew. In 1923 Saracens were regularly running four fifteens and another fifteen, formed shortly afterwards, prompted the club to seek larger accommodation. By 1928 they were settled at Firs Farm, Winchmore Hill, and a happy period of expansion in the thirties was arrested by the double blow of war and notice from Edmonton Council that the ground was to be developed for housing. Forced to seek new premises, Saracens alighted at Bramley Road Sports Ground in the early days of World War Two, and there they have remained.

In the first post-war decade, the club invariably won more matches than were lost in each season. Dr. John Steeds, a hooker, became the first England player capped directly from Saracens, and Vic Harding, recruited appropriately from St. Marylebone GS, began playing in the club's pack in 1952–53. In a distinguished playing career he won three Cambridge Blues, became Saracens' most-capped international player and led the club to its first appearance in a Middlesex Sevens final in 1958. Among the leading lights in the '60s and '70s were England cap George Sheriff, Mike Alder, a prolific points-scorer, Ian Player and Peter Cadle.

The club's drive for excellence, started in 1974 with the establishment of a forward planning committee, paid handsome dividends in 1988-89 when Saracens achieved promotion to Courage League Division One with a 100% record and John Buckton, a forceful centre, became their first back to play for England.

Above: *Stuart Wilson, Gregg Botterman, Andy Roda: the Saracen's front row get steaming mad. Would you buy a used gumshield from these men?*
Above left: *Saracens 12, Gloucester 12; 11 January 1992. Despite being totally outnumbered and having his ankles held (just out of shot), Lee Adamson – the author's hero – wins terrific line-out ball against an out-classed and demoralised Gloucester pack.*
Opposite page: *Saracens fixture card. Carbon dated 1881.*

FACING FORWARDS

No 11: Justyn Cassell

Position: Open-side flanker **Age:** 25 **Ht:** 6'3" **Wt:** 15 st

There are times to tell your boss when to shove the job. This man can time the moment to perfection. The ideal scenario runs like this: get selected for the England B tour to New Zealand. Approach the boss for time off; get turned down and so hand in resignation. Follow it so far? Sounds like a fairly normal thing to do, yeah. Wait, because here comes the *pièce de resistance*. The week after your principled action, you then get sent off against Bath. Normal suspension would put you out of the tour. Oh, dear. No tour and no job. Fortunately the disciplinary committee were lenient and Justyn went on tour.
One of the finds of last season and a great future in prospect.

Clubs
Marlow
Hobbies
Water-skiing, my wife
Hero
Peter Winterbottom
(I was just out of short trousers when he won first cap)
Worst game
Bath 1991, I can still see that digit of doom pointing to the dressing-room
Least enjoyable aspect
Having forwards leave their studded signature all over your back after a ruck
Attitude to fitness
Do it but hate it
Best tour
Marlow to Vancouver 1990
Best tour story
CENSORED (what goes on tour stays on tour)
Least favourite roommate
Kinsey, O'Leary, Dear – three of the biggest bouncers in the world.
They gave me a fearful kicking in Perth, 1991, when on London tour. My crime? Snoring. Mind you, it did cure the snoring

Favourite drink
Boddingtons
Favourite food
Cantonese. I'm a dab hand at the Yellow Pages and can rustle up a good Chinese restuarant within a few minutes
Favourite film
'The Hand That Rocks The Cradle'
Favourite newspaper
Daily Telegraph
Opinion media
Do they come to Saracens?
Drinking capacity
Diminished drastically.
I slide down the wall slowly and quietly much earlier in the evening than I used to
Champion drinkers in side
The second-row, Lee Adamson and Mark Langley
Motto
Play fair (honestly)
Ambitions
England, British Lions, then I can get on with life
Most interesting thing about myself
I'm a Christian
Who I would most liked to have been
Clint Eastwood

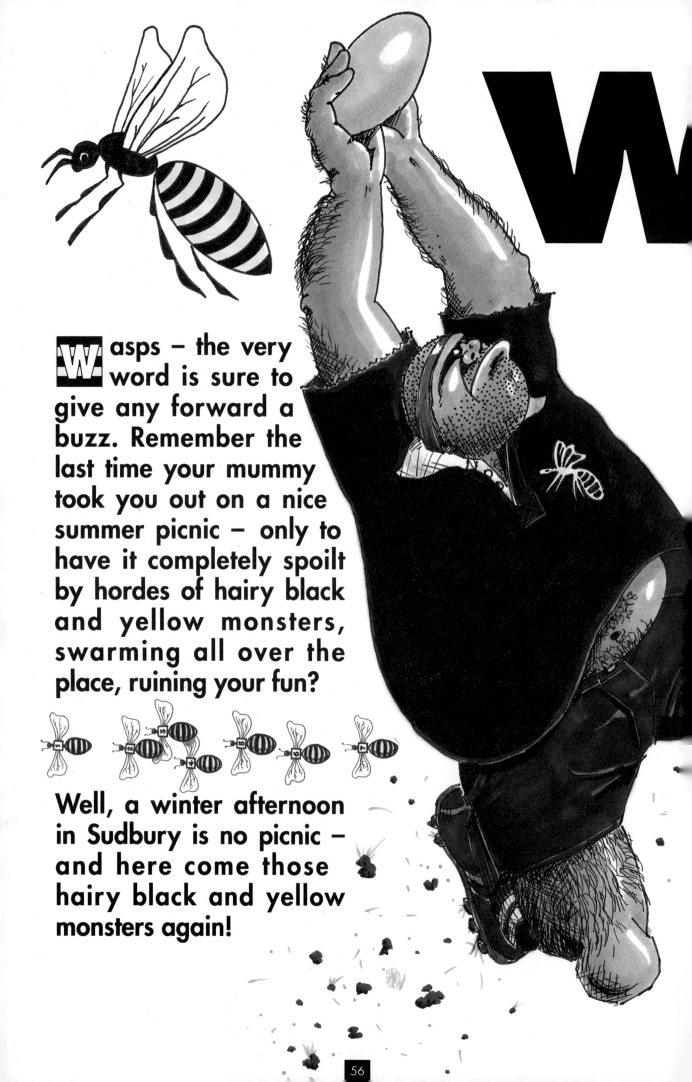

Wasps – the very word is sure to give any forward a buzz. Remember the last time your mummy took you out on a nice summer picnic – only to have it completely spoilt by hordes of hairy black and yellow monsters, swarming all over the place, ruining your fun?

Well, a winter afternoon in Sudbury is no picnic – and here come those hairy black and yellow monsters again!

Where the hell are they?

The Wasps will spoil your day at Wasps Football Ground, Repton Avenue, Sudbury, Middlesex. Tel: 081-902 4220.

1. The Swan
2. The Mitre
3. The Dog and Duck
4. Norfolk Arms

Stations:
A. North Wembley
B. Sudbury & Harrow Road
C. Sudbury Town
D. Wembley Central

Where's the bar?

CLUB HOUSE

EATON AVENUE

Who scores all the points?

(Swat this lot before dealing with the rest)

Leading scorers in the League 1991/92
S. Pilgrim (2 tries, 6 cons, 27 pens) 101
C. Oti (5 tries) 20, H. Davies (1 try, 2 pens, 2 dg) 16, D. Hopley (2 tries) 8
Wasps' 177 League points included 18 tries.

How did they do last year?

PLAYED 12 • WON 6 • DRAWN 0 • LOST 6
Points for: 177 • Points against: 180
7TH IN COURAGE LEAGUE ONE

Where are the nearest pubs?

See the map.

What else?

Founded 1867.
Second XV:
Vandals

CHANGE STRIP

League History: First Division since 1987.
League Honours: First Division Champions 1990.
Cup Honours: Finalists 1986, 1987.

Wasps were founded in 1867 by a group of old Merchant Taylors' boys who were medical students at London hospitals. The name followed the fashion set by contemporaries from other public schools – the Gipsies of Tonbridge and the Nomads of Marlborough for example – and predictably the club's original colours were black and amber hoops.

By January 1871 they were prominent enough to receive an invitation to the formation of the RFU. But Wasps' committee members went to the wrong hostelry and, enjoying the fare and service, the laid-back officials never honoured their appointment. Thus Wasps missed a listing as founder members of the Union.

The current colours with the wasp emblem were endorsed in 1873 and five years later the club's first international, Dr. J.M. Biggs of University College Hospital, played for England.

Generous hospitality is permanently associated with Wasps. During its roving existence between 1867 and 1923, when the present site at Sudbury was purchased with an RFU loan, the club's grounds were invariably adjacent to licensed premises. Today, of course, Wasps entertain guests at the splendid club pavilion erected in 1963.

Until the last war, Wasps ranked as a minor club. There was an unbeaten season in 1930–31 when convincing wins in the West Country prompted one pundit to conclude that they were not merely pikes among the minnows of London rugby. Then during the war years, Neville Compton kept club football alive at Sudbury, staging regular matches for servicemen on leave and players in reserved occupations.

Compton's initiative paid dividends in peacetime when demobbed rugby men made a beeline for Sudbury. Wasps won the Middlesex Sevens in 1948 and the club's stock rose rapidly in the '50s. Peter Yarranton, recent president of the RFU whose name has been synonymous with Wasps for the past forty years, and

Wasps 1991–92: Back Row: P. Harding (Touch Judge), M. Friday, J. Allan, P. Carroll (Team Secretary), I. Dunston, P. Hopley, D. Hopley, D. Ryan, S. O'Leary, R. Kinsey, M. White, J. Probyn, G. Holmes, R. Lozowski, P. Moyle (Coach), A. Buzza, P. Fox (Fitness Coach).
Front Row: M. Harris, P. Green, G. Childs, S. Pilgrim, J. Langley (Manager), M. Rigby (Captain), M. Green (President), S. Bates, H. Davies, C. Oti, T. Herbert.

Bob Stirling, captain of the England Triple-Crown team in 1954, were among nearly two dozen Wasps who won international honours during the decade.

Ted Woodward and Ron Syrett were brothers-in-law who played for England and Wasps during this period, and the outstanding fly-half Richard Sharp travelled from Oxford University to play for the club in 1960–61 when, under Peter Yarranton, seven defeats in 35 games marked one of the club's most successful seasons.

Thereafter Wasps slipped into relative decline before results began to improve in the late '70s. The arrival at Sudbury of Roger Uttley in 1979–80 was a boost to the club and in the following seasons, shored up by big guns such as Mark Taylor of New Zealand, Nick Stringer, Richard Cardus, Nigel Melville, Jeff Probyn and Paul Rendall, Wasps established themselves among the leading English sides.

A significant development in the mid-'80s has been the Cambridge connection whereby more than half a dozen of the University's backs have graduated to senior rugby at Sudbury. The blend of attacking rugby founded on basic skills learned at Cambridge by Rob Andrew, Huw Davies and Kevin Simms, to name but three, has benefited Wasps (and England). And with evergreens Probyn and Rendall to prop the scrums, Wasps have given their loyal

followers plenty to cheer about since the launch of the Courage Leagues in 1987. They were second in 1988, third in 1989, and in 1990, under Rob Andrew, the club reached its pinnacle, winning the First Division.

Above: *Wasps 20, Harlequins 6: 16 November 1991. Paddy Dunston's not going to let anybody else go to the ball, as Alan Simmons and Darren Malloy discover to their cost. Dean Ryan (N° 8) looks on, astonished.*
Opposite page: *Wasps trashing Harlequins is nothing new. Wasps 14, Harlequins 5: Middlesex Sevens programme, 1948.*

FACING FORWARDS

No 12: Jeffrey Probyn

Position: Prop **Age:** 36 **Ht:** 5' 10½" **Wt:** 15½ st

After Jeffrey Alan Probyn was born they threw away the mould. There is no other prop of the same shape in the world. Oh, Jeffrey may look the same as all the others – not too far removed from Guy the Gorilla at London Zoo – but appearances are deceptive. Heineken should sign him up for one of their advertisements, because Jeffrey reaches the parts in scrummages that no other prop can reach. His shoulders go where they shouldn't, his neck sinks into flesh that it is has no right to encounter, and his arms entwine the opposition like an octopus. Jeff began his career in the centre which explains the occasional brainstorm when he forsakes everything prop forwards the world over stand for – in other words, 'the ball is ours and those nancy boys in the threequarters are not having it' – and tries to run. Didn't win his first cap until the age of 31, and he is now the cornerstone of the England pack. Jeff plays with indecent vigour for a man of his advanced years.

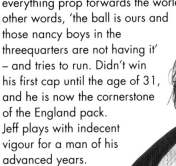

Hobbies
Shooting, sailing, fishing. Used to do them a lot until I discovered rugby

Heroes
Fran Cotton, Gareth Edwards (delusions of being swift and skilful), Gary Pearce, who was playing for England when I was down among the boozers and bruisers in junior rugby

Best game
Against France, any one of several in the last few years

Worst game
Every night 'Flower of Scotland' cuts deep into my dreams. Murrayfield, 1990, the Grand Slam is ours. Och, nae, it isn't, says a little Scottish voice, and he was right

Best opponent
Paul Rendall. I know we have a pledge to mention each other in public whenever we can and I know we both play for the same club. I did spend five years at Richmond playing against him though. To stop me hitting him Judge got me to join Wasps

Most enjoyable moment
Wales, Twickenham, 1990. First scrum, their put in, we drove them off the ball. The game was as good as over

Opinion new fitness regime
As an international player, no problem; as a former drinking player, horrific

Opinion of props
All shapes and sizes. Strange to relate, we all enjoy running with the ball. Problem is we have little sense of direction. If you tied our ankles to a 50-metre ball of string in the middle of the pitch by the end of the game we'd be running in a 3-metre circle

Best tour
South Africa Centenary Tour 1989. It was great to play alongside rather than against certain nationalities. I even got on well with the French

Best tour story
CENSORED

Least favourite roommate
Myself

Most embarrassing moment
Wales, 1988. Forgot to concentrate at a scrum and next thing I knew I was up out of the scrum and looking at the West Car Park. Only time I've ever had flying lessons from another prop

Relationship with referees
Symbiotic

Favourite drink
Whatever is free

Drinking capacity
It depends if Geoff Cooke is watching

Champion drinker
Judge Rendall

Motto
Do It To Them Before They Do It To You

Biggest compliment ever paid
Being hit by the opposition second-row. It means you've got them worried

Most interesting thing about myself
My shoulders

Who I would most liked to have been
Duke of Westminster

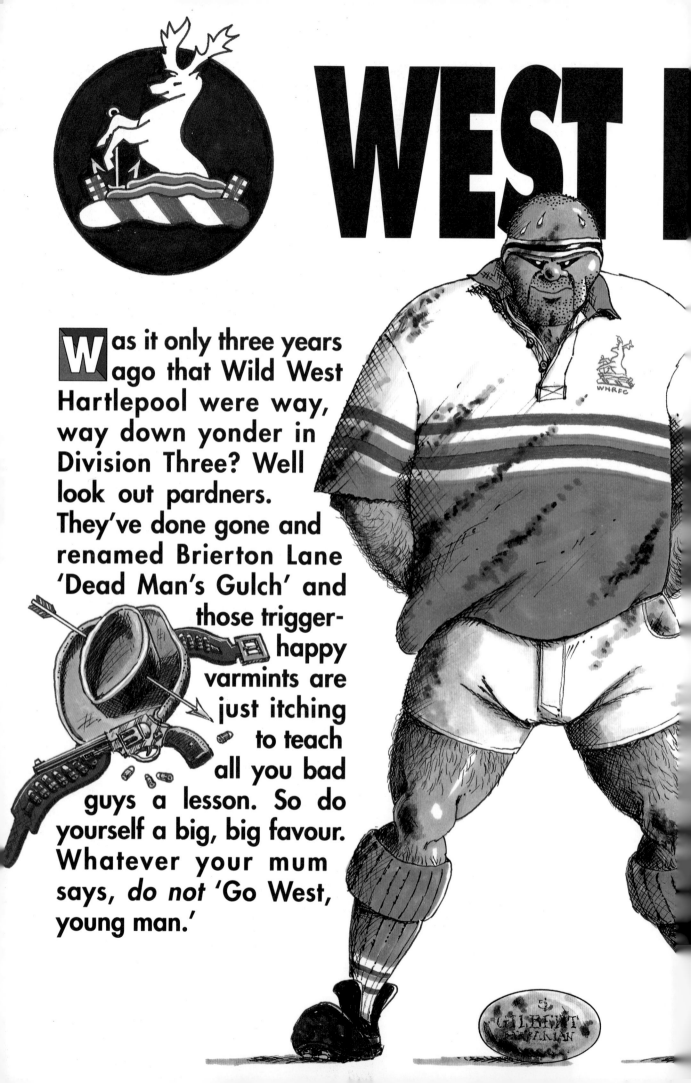

WEST

Was it only three years ago that Wild West Hartlepool were way, way down yonder in Division Three? Well look out pardners. They've done gone and renamed Brierton Lane 'Dead Man's Gulch' and those trigger-happy varmints are just itching to teach all you bad guys a lesson. So do yourself a big, big favour. Whatever your mum says, *do not* 'Go West, young man.'

ARTLEPOOL

Where the hell are they?

The West live up East in Brierton Lane, Hartlepool, Cleveland.
Telephone: 0429 272640.

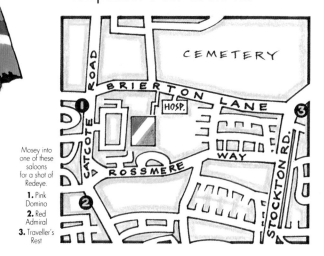

Mosey into one of these saloons for a shot of Redeye.
1. Pink Domino
2. Red Admiral
3. Traveller's Rest

Where's the bar?

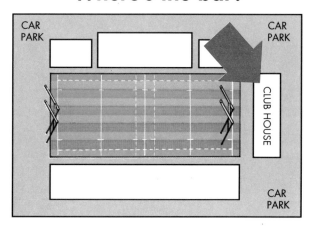

Who scores all the points?
(Fill 'em full of lead.)

Leading scorers in the League 1991/92
J. Stabler (2 tries, 16 cons, 26 pens) 118
J. Wrigley (7 tries) 28
A. Brown (5 tries) 20, P. Evans (3 tries) 12
Penalty tries (3) 12
West Hartlepool's 244 League points included 33 tries.

How did they do last year?

PLAYED 12 • WON 11 • DRAWN 0 • LOST 1
Points for: 244 • Points against: 89
2ND IN COURAGE LEAGUE TWO

Where are the nearest pubs?
See the map.

What else?

Founded 1881.
Nickname: 'West.'
Second XV: Stags.

CHANGE STRIP

League History: Second Division 1991–92;
Third Division 1987–91.

League Honours: Third Division Champions 1991.

West Hartlepool trace their origins back to 1875–76 when matches were played at Belle Vue. West struggled to establish a viable club in the early years and a severe leg injury sustained by one of their leading forwards in a match in 1880 was the catalyst that prompted the club to disband.

Four years later however, a fresh attempt to develop the club at Foggy Furze was made and, under the captaincy of W.H. Humphreys, more than a dozen matches were completed. Humphreys was an admirable forward who later served Durham county rugby as an administrator, and in 1893 was invited to referee Wales' internationals against Scotland and Ireland.

The club was on the move again in 1887, this time to the Victoria Ground where West stayed for twenty fruitful playing years until financial problems beset the club, forcing another disbandment in 1908. During this period, seven West Hartlepool men won international caps, the club won both the Durham senior cup and league, and regularly supplied players for the Durham side which dominated the English county championship, winning five outright titles between 1900 and 1909.

Jack Taylor was the most distinguished club player of this era. He was rated the outstanding threequarter in England at the turn of the century and his eleven internationals included one as captain of England. A prodigious kicker, his three dropped goals were the major contribution to West's famous win against the Barbarians in 1902. The victory

West Hartlepool, 1991–92: Back row: *P. Whitelock, G. Evans, P. Pook, J. Dixon, A. Brown, P. Evans, S. Cassidy, P. Lancaster.*
Front row: *J. Wrigley, G. Armstrong, K. Oliphant, S. Mitchell, J. Stabler (Captain), P. Hodder, P. Robinson, C. Lee, D. Cook.* ***Mascot:*** *Elliot Stead.*

really put Taylor's team on the rugby map. Fixture invitations arrived from Scottish, Irish and Welsh teams, and for the international against Wales in 1903, three West Hartlepool players were included in England's XV.

The demise of West in 1908 led directly to the foundation of the Hartlepool United Football Club, who commandeered the Victoria Ground. So, when the West Hartlepool rugby club was reformed in 1911, matches were again staged at Foggy Furze before new premises were leased on the Clarence Road. Here the club stayed until 1965, and here a teenaged Durham schoolboy, Carl Aarvold, made his first-class debut in 1924–25.

Although studies at Cambridge and commitments as a barrister in the south restricted his appearances for West, Aarvold – later Sir Carl Aarvold, high court judge and Recorder of London – was the club's outstanding product between the wars. Capped 16 times for England and captain on seven occasions, in 1930 he became the only Englishman to date to lead the British Lions to victory in a Test against New Zealand.

Milestones in the club's history since the last war include the move in 1965 to the present headquarters at Brierton Lane, and the celebration of a happy centenary season in which the famous Whetton twins from New Zealand featured in West's colours. Terry Arthur, whose father was a stalwart of the club in the '20s and '30s, was capped by England from Wasps in 1966, but he began his senior rugby at West Hartlepool whilst a pupil of the local grammar school.

Now the club is riding high again after promotion to Division One of the Courage Leagues, though the euphoria of last season's achievements was overshadowed by the tragic death of West's popular lock, John Howe.

Above: Sale 13, West 15; 21 December 1991. A ferocious maul takes place at Sale's Heywood Road ground. The players involved have failed to notice that the ball has been in touch for several minutes.
Above left: West v. Gosforth, 14 March 1992. Geordies totally thrashed, 13–7.
Opposite page: West's captain John Stabler kicks an opposing back into touch.

FACING FORWARDS

No 13: Paul Evans

Position: Blindside/N°8 **Age:** 25 **Ht:** 6'3"
Wt: 16 st (has lost weight in close season – how times have changed)

You don't know them and, by the time they've finished with you, you certainly don't want to know them. From a strange, far-flung outpost on the north-east coast, some weird bodies are entering the First Division for the first time. And they don't come any stranger than Paul Evans. On the surface, he's pleasant, articulate and entirely normal. Dig beneath the surface and you find a man that has formed a Chipmunk Club (don't ask me why), goes by the name of Ninja or Biff (any *Viz* reader apparently will know what this means) and once almost drowned after diving into a pool in America when he was drunk. Sounds daft enough for anyone: this man was actually employed as the lifesaver. You have been warned.

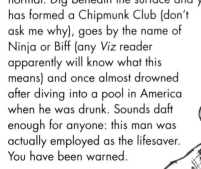

Previous clubs
Loughborough University, Bridlington
Nicknames
Ninja; Biff
Hobbies
Music; over 4,000 albums
Best game
Texas Tournament, 1991.
Teams from South America and States.
I was playing for Houston.
We won and Texas went wild
Most enjoyable aspect of game
Respect of peers
Least enjoyable
Thugs. More of them at junior level
Best tour
West Hartlepool to America, 1990
Best tour story
Not censored – read on.
24-hour bar opposite hotel
in New Orleans, frequented by winos,
pimps and West players.
Felt quite at home.
Did the 24-hour stint.
Returned to hotel, staggered past
committee who were just getting up,
plunged into pool,
one of us was violently sick,
scooped it up and ate it

Most embarrassing moment
On train during miners' strike.
Fell asleep. Woke up
thinking it was the table leg my knee
was nestling against.
It wasn't. Opened eyes to see I was
surrounded by policemen
en route to duty. I got away with it – just
Favourite drink
Cider
Favourite food
Seafood
Favourite film
'Streetfighter'
Favourite paper
Daily Telegraph
Drinking capacity
Depends who's paying
Champion drinkers in side
John Dixon and Antony Elwine
Biggest insult ever received
Is that an eclipse
or has Evans's backside just gone by?
**Most interesting thing
about myself**
Founder of Chipmunk Club
**Who I would most liked
to have been**
Rasputin